Homeschool 2020

Lessons For Bright Children From a Dark Year

Written By Sasha Yevelev

Design by Ed Yevelev

ISBN: 978-1-7367326-0-1

CONTENTS

ACKNOWLEDGMENTS.

I have always found this section of a book to be somewhat obvious. Of course the author owes his partner and family a huge debt of gratitude for their patience. But damn, do I ever. Mila, thank you for allowing me to turn our home into a laboratory of learning, and a castle of chaos. Thank you for supporting - and frankly - tolerating me.

Dov, I hope one day you will understand the boundless, indescribable love I feel for you. This is all for you, and because of you.

Ed, thank you for bringing this book visually to life! I am so lucky to have you in my corner.

To my homeschool kids and their families.
Thank you for inspiring me, for putting your trust in me, and for allowing me to captain this unexpected, uncharted, offbeat voyage.

To my family.

Mila, my foundation.
Dov, my motivation.
Ira, my fascination.

My parents, Dina and Igor.
My brothers, Ed and Gary.

To my homeschool kids, my inspiration.

"I can't go on forever, and I don't really want to try. So who can I trust to run the factory when I leave, and take care of the Oompa Loompas for me? Not a grown up. A grown up would want to do everything his own way, not mine. So that's why I decided a long time ago that I had to find a child. A very honest, loving child, to whom I could tell all my most precious candy making secrets."

-Willy Wonka

Charlie and The Chocolate Factory, 1971

WHY.

My homeschool kids know two things for sure. One: If they spill water, I will bury them in a shallow, unmarked grave. Two: My favorite question is "Why?"

We only have one chance to make a first impression. And if the "shallow, unmarked grave" just convinced you that I am a horrible human being, you might be asking why I opened a book about homeschooling five-, six- and seven- year old children with such a distasteful threat.

The way I see it, if I made you ask "Why?", then we're already off in the right direction.

As you read this book, you will learn that I have a peculiar sense of humor. I am not shy about sharing this humor with my kids, because I believe that kids are much more perceptive and capable than adults give them credit for. Moreover, if we cannot delight in some dark humor, especially as we look back on 2020, then we are taking ourselves way too seriously.

My kids know that I have not yet dug any shallow, unmarked graves, and that none of their peers have gone missing. They have never seen my shovel (I have one, I assure them). This, despite several glasses of water being tipped over. My kids also know that shallow is the opposite of deep, and they know that un- is a prefix meaning not. And they fell in love with the word peculiar ever since it was part of our vocabulary lesson a few months ago.

The quarantine was announced in mid-March, 2020. My son's school went dark for two weeks, scrambling to roll out a distance learning strategy. What they came back with was three, 30-minute zoom classes, four days a week. It was the early days of Zoom, and I didn't know what to expect. My gut told me that it would be a flop. After closely monitoring the classes for a couple of days, it became clear to me that this type of learning was a disaster. If there was an immediate silver lining to the pandemic, it's that we as parents now had full transparency into what, and how, our children were being taught. This was also a very delicate and precious a time in my son's development, and I feared consequences far beyond a bad academic year. We had no idea how long the pandemic would last. With everything closing down left and right, and with very little information available, I imagined what the upshot of home confinement and school via screen could be. I suddenly saw an apocalyptic vision of my son as a bleary-eyed, isolated, jittery, depressed and fearful child. Without hesitation, I pulled my son out of school, and fully committed myself to homeschooling him for the rest of the year.

I didn't blame the teachers. I assumed everyone was approaching the situation with their best intentions. It's simply that an in-person classroom curriculum cannot be literally transposed to a small screen. You have to start from scratch, and come up with a whole new approach to engage and motivate kids. You need to be flexible and innovative. You have to improvise. Imagine an experienced kindergarten teacher, who has been operating the same way for 25 years. Now, suddenly, they not only have to learn a whole new technology - they have to reinvent how they teach altogether. It's a nearly impossible ask.

Instead of wallowing in annoyance and frustration, I decided to pay myself the tuition, and to prove that I can do it better. My mission was clear: Take ownership. Maintain a sense of normalcy amidst the crisis and dread. Create the kind of experience for my son that would enrich him, and make him excited to greet each new day. I sat down and brainstormed a list of ideas and topics that would engage my 5 year old. I didn't let the perfect get in the way of the good. There was no time to waste.

WHO.

Who am I? I am not a professional educator, but I have always been good with kids. I don't have vivid memories of my early childhood, but I know I inherited a lot of my creativity from my father. When I was 5 years old, he built me a robot. That robot slept with me, dined with me, played chess with me.

I got a lot of real-world childcare experience from being the older brother of twin boys. As a teenager, I spent two summers being a camp counselor. I felt very comfortable in that role, and I relished organizing and challenging my kids. There was a legendary push-up contest where my bunk of boys (after training for two weeks) defeated a tough rival bunk. The hero of the tournament was a pudgy kid who had lacked confidence and self esteem at the start of the session. It was a glorious moment for him, and I never forgot it. In college, I taught chess to kids to earn some extra lunch money. In my twenties, I spent a few years studying and performing improv. The ability to improvise is crucial when working with children. Some of the games and ideas I learned as an improviser are an integral part of my homeschool curriculum.

For the past 15 years, I've been a wedding and family photographer, honing my ability to manage kids in stressful environments. For the last nine years, I have been a devotee of the CrossFit method of fitness. CrossFit workouts are something I do almost daily, and I supplement with yoga. CrossFit has helped me become a stronger, healthier, more confident person, and my son Dov grew up around our gym. His competitive personality and love of sports is probably due in no small part to my wife and I modeling this behavior for him. Since he was a baby, we've been constantly bringing him into an environment where people find joy and community in fitness. The push and challenge of CrossFit reminds me of wrestling in high school. I was not a great wrestler, and I only stuck with it for a couple years. However, it was a highly formative experience for me. The feeling of being completely and utterly exhausted after a practice. The feeling of pushing yourself to, and past, your limits. The feeling of accomplishment, and measurable and obvious progress.

Taken together, those are my credentials. Parents have often asked me during this time: "Where do you get your ideas?" The truth is, I don't really know. Most of the time they just appear in my mind, it feels right, and I run with it. My guess is that it's some sort of mental engine built by the sum of my past experiences. My brain churns out ideas when pressure is applied.

Kids love games. They connect with adults who exhibit playfulness and maybe a bit of mischief. I've always been able to look at a kid with a glint in my eye, like, "Hey, I bet you can't do this!". A little smirk. A joke. The ability to turn a boring everyday object into something cool and desirable. A stick on the ground: "I bet you can't jump over this!" A bandana: "Hey, let's play capture the flag!" Some sidewalk chalk: "Let's design the world's greatest hopscotch!" There are millions of five-star reviewed fancy educational toys on Amazon, but observing my son for the last six years has taught me that kids don't need fancy toys for development. They just need our creativity, and more importantly, our full attention. My first epiphany came early, when my son was just a year old. He got lots of those fancy developmental toys for his birthday, but he loved nothing more than playing with lids, empty plastic jars, and crumpling up brown paper bags.

HOW.

Back to March. After pulling the plug on school, I immediately began a homeschool curriculum. In many ways, I was building on what I had already been doing for the last few years to educate my son. I had always been an opportunistic educator, so I knew intuitively how to invent games and challenges. In some ways, though, I was feeling my way forward in the dark. After all, it's one thing to engage your kid in the car or on the playground. It's quite another to suddenly have to consider a curriculum to replace a 7-hour school day.

One thing I knew right away is that I wanted to avoid busywork. I've always had a distaste for school worksheets, especially for K level. Color these triangles blue! Match each kitten with his ball of yarn! Do these 50 ridiculously easy math problems. It's just time-consuming busywork that still has to be supervised and quality-controlled by parents. Worksheets would not be a tool in my curriculum. I would not assign homework outside of the lessons.

The Green Schoolhouse

After a couple weeks of homeschool, I looked around and realized that the parents of my son's peers could really use a hand during this pandemic insanity. I imagined that if I were working a full time job and juggling kids from home, I'd be really grateful if someone reached out to me and said "Hey, I can provide an hour a day of really high quality educational content for your kid. This will not be the typical Zoom school snoozefest. I will not only buy you an hour of time to yourself, I will guarantee that your kid will be engaged in a positive and constructive way." So I decided to put it to the test. Together with my son, I launched an educational program for kids called The Green Schoolhouse. I wanted this to be a win-win. I benefit by getting ideas across to my kid. I help out other parents. I give other kids a sense of badly-needed community. I give my son the opportunity to "co-host" the program and to feel empowered.

I had staged a puppet show for a Halloween party a couple years earlier, and it had been a big success. I decided to dust off the old puppets and make them a centerpiece of the program. I had a simple "dad" puppet. Blue shirt, yellow tie. So I dressed myself like the puppet, and called myself "Papa", while the puppet was "Puppet Papa". I also had a red devil puppet, which worked really well as an antagonist. Dov dubbed him "Evil Bad". I figured playing these puppets off each other would make for great theater for the kids, and would help get ideas across. I set up a makeshift studio using some of my photography props, and off we went.

Our first episode was called "The Golden Rule", and it was all about treating people the way you want to be treated. We went on to do over 70 shows - one every single weekday, well into June. We covered dozens of topics. Among them, "The Five Senses", "Rock, Paper, Scissors", "Nutrition", and a whole week dedicated to probability. Dov and I even created and mailed "probability boxes" to the participating kids, so that they could use the same probability tools that we were using during the lessons.

I threw everything and the kitchen sink at these lessons. I battle tested many different ideas and tools. Puppets (obviously). Costumes. Themes. Wigs. Lighting effects. Lots of Socratic Method. Guest stars, like a childrens' musician and my very artistic brother (the cover designer for this book) who taught a virtual art lesson. The Green Schoolhouse started as an experiment, and something that I thought *could* be a benefit to my son and his peers. It really exceeded my expectations and became something much more: An important part of our routine, and a way to stay sane and committed during the disorienting first few months of shelter-in-place. It also became the foundation for what would come next. The Green Schoolhouse lessons and probability boxes are still available on the website https://www.thegreenschoolhouse.com/. The full set of lessons is archived on The Green Schoolhouse YouTube Channel. (If you have a print copy of this book, just go to YouTube and search "Green Schoolhouse").

Planning for the Fall

It occurred to me at some point in the late spring that in-person school might not come back in the fall. I needed to think about the bigger picture. Could I homeschool my son for a full school year? What would that look like? I realized that the academic part of it was not going to be sufficient. I would need to build a cohort of kids around him, so that he could learn in a group environment and fulfill the social aspect of learning as well. Many parents realised the same thing. These cohorts would eventually come to be called "pods", and I would become, I suppose, a Podfather. (Warning, dad jokes ahead!)

We were lucky to have an outdoor space across the street from our house. A space where kids could still run around and get exercise despite the quarantine. During the first few months of shelter-in-place, this would be the place where Dov would hone his bike skills, the place where we would design those epic hopscotches and obstacle courses. Our little outdoor corner of salvation from the pandemic. I knew that this space and adjacent playground would be crucial tools in our homeschool efforts.

WHAT.

There was a time when I would drop my son off at school in the morning, and pick him up in the evening. Everything in between was sort of a black box. Surely he was learning something, progressing, improving. But the transparency was not there. How much of his school day was busywork? How much was simply childcare? How much of it was spent watching videos? If I knew exactly what he was up to all day, would I really approve? What would I do differently? I recognize that this mindset sounds quiet helicopter-y, and that I recently heard Jerry Seinfeld say that the best thing his parents did for him was to treat him with benign neglect. Implication: he turned out fine. But I fully admit that I am of the generation of helicopter parents, and I decided to not get hung up debating the ethics in my own mind.

If I had a blank canvas to teach my son anything I wanted, what would I focus on? What's really important in today's world?

This book is a compendium of those things that made the cut. These are lessons, topics, games, activities and approaches that I found to be most effective. I have been homeschooling my son from March 2020 to June, and then, after a short summer break, from early August through mid-February (as of the writing of this book). After these months, I have a six year old whose level of math is probably on par with that of an average fourth or fifth grade public school student. He's adding and subtracting large two digit numbers comfortably in his head. He's adding and subtracting thousands and millions on paper/whiteboard. He's easily doing multiplication and division into the teens. He can look at a data set and draw conclusions. He understands concepts of geometry, angles and shapes, how to calculate the area of two- and three- dimensional figures. He understands basic exponents and square root. He understands line graphs, pie charts and bar charts. He is reading comfortably, if not always willingly, and perfecting his spelling day by day. He plays chess. He's an eager public speaker and performer. He exhibits leadership and naturally mentors other kids. Athletically, he's coordinated, confident and strong. In many emotional ways, he's still a six year old. But I could never have imagined that we would make this kind of progress on all fronts.

The main purpose of this book is to share my experience with you. I stand in solidarity with my fellow parents. So long as the schools stay completely or partially shut, the buck will be passed to us to educate our children. I want you to learn from my mistakes and successes, so that you can use these tools to help your children. So that you never again have to be "out of ideas" about how to motivate or entertain your kid.

But I'd be lying if I said that was the only purpose of this book. I also have a selfish reason for writing it. I want it to be a memoir and a monument of sorts. I want to leave something behind from this crazy year we all just lived through. Before the pandemic, I was a photographer, and a motivated father. The pandemic forced me to build an addition to that house. The pandemic gave me the push. And I've bottled that push here for you in these pages.

HOW TO USE THIS BOOK.

Remember I mentioned CrossFit above? Crossfit is a program that allows athletes to scale their workouts based on several levels of ability. Some gyms use "conditioning", "development" and "competition" to describe the different possible challenge levels in a workout. Some gyms use Levels 1, 2, 3. Some simply use Rx (or "as prescribed") or Scaled (lower weight, less challenging). Think of it as a similar system to green circle, blue square, black diamond in skiing. For example, Level 1 might call for a 95 pound barbell; Level 2 - 115 pounds; Level 3 / Rx / Competition - 135. I have used a similar approach here. Many lessons and activities contained in this book are scalable. Once your child gets the basics, I've included some options to scale up for greater challenge.

The chapters are not necessarily sequential. You can skip around and take detours.

Is this book only for K and 1st Grade students? Hardly. Many of the concepts I teach here are quite advanced. It's simply a question of how you teach them. I honestly believe that there are many things in this book that you can impart to middle school, and even high school kids.

You don't have to worry about your child's assigned grade level. The pandemic has wreaked havoc on those distinctions. All you have to do is honestly assess your child's abilities and pay attention to the feedback they are giving you. They can begin a lesson at a very scaled approach, and then slowly but surely you can increase and push further towards the higher levels. This kind of flexible approach works beautifully in CrossFit to eventually get beginner athletes to a place where they can achieve high performance. I battle tested this approach because my homeschool pod had children of all varying abilities. Two kids might both be five years old, but they could be worlds apart as far as their academic and physical abilities. By scaling my lessons and challenges to each child, I gave each one the opportunity to succeed at their own pace. Small wins are super important for kids. They build confidence and help bridge the child over to the next level.

Here's a quick, concrete example (I'll dive deeper into this later in the book). The monkey bars are one of my favorite implements on the playground. Level 1 of doing monkey bars might be just hanging on one bar for as long as possible, without letting go; getting comfortable with the feeling of supporting your body with your arms and the friction and burn of the metal on your skin. Level 2 might be moving forward one bar at a time. Level 3 would be skipping a bar with each movement, and a Level 3 challenge could be going back and forth as many times as possible without letting go.

The Krav Maga Approach

Krav Maga is an Israeli martial art, invented by Hungarian immigrant Imi Lichtenfeld in the 1940's. The philosophy behind Krav Maga is to take simple and effective techniques from a variety of fighting disciplines, and to employ them in combination. This strips away the pomp and circumstance of many martial arts, to create a common sense, easily teachable, extremely practical self defense system. It's no wonder that the Israeli Army and many other military and law enforcement organizations have adopted it as part of their training.

I first took Krav Maga classes nearly 20 years ago, but I will never forget a demonstration by our Israeli instructor, Danny Zelig. He had been a commando in the elite Golani Brigade unit, so he was the real deal. The class I'll never forget is the one where he taught us what to do if you are assaulted by a gang of aggressors. Many against one. Make no mistake, he said. You will be lucky to come out of this alive. You do not follow any conventional rules or ideas. Take what you can get. If they have long hair, pull it. If you can reach their eyes, gouge them with your fingers. If they have piercings, rip them out. *You have to get crrrrazy*, he emphasized, with that almost guttural, unmistakable Israeli "rrrrr". You are outnumbered and in grave danger. So you must make your attackers understand that you are like an animal. They may kill you, but make it clear that before that happens, you're going to take one of them with you.

Krav Maga teaches that when the odds are stacked against you, you have to dispense with formulas and rigid ideas. You have to know your basic principles, and then you have to improvise to survive. Have you figured out where I'm going with this? Why have I introduced such bloody imagery into a book about educating children? I suppose I could have found a different analogy, but honestly, let's agree: it's a pretty useful lesson on how to survive a street fight. More importantly, I've modeled my entire approach on the Krav Maga idea. While public schools have been too rigid and bureaucratic to navigate pandemic education, homeschool worked because I dispensed with rigid, conventional ideas. I improvised and operated nimbly.

The Whiteboard

I have also included in this book lots of actual photographs and screenshots of lessons that I did on the whiteboard for my students. The whiteboard has been an incredibly valuable teaching tool for me. It's a way to quickly convey and modify information. It also encourages the kids to *want* to come up to the whiteboard, and to use their own little white boards when they are given a chance. My kids eagerly jump up to the whiteboard to demonstrate a concept, or provide an answer to the rest of the class. They want to be the ones holding the marker in their hands.

Brainstorm

Early on, I introduced Dov and all the kids to the concept of brainstorming. This is a critical arrow in the education quiver that I use over and over in my lessons. The way I introduced "brainstorm" was to deconstruct this compound word, and to ask them to imagine a storm. Wind is blowing, leaves are flying around, water is pouring down from the sky. It's intense. There's a charge. There's a lot of energy in the air. That's how I encourage my kids to brainstorm. Except instead of leaves and rain and wind, it's our ideas flying out of our brains. I summon their energy when we brainstorm. I become very animated, pointing, gesticulating, calling on people, getting excited about each idea, punctuating suggestions with an emphatic "Yes!". I make sure to write down *all* ideas on the whiteboard in some form. You cannot discourage during this critical time. You have to find a way to fashion even bad or non sequitur suggestions into something usable. I work the kids up to a fever pitch until the whiteboard is filled with suggestions. I make sure everyone felt heard. If a student has been shy to throw out ideas, I ask them what they think about the ones already on the board. Perhaps we can add something? Or maybe we can embellish an idea together? Hold their hand, walk them through it. Make them feel valued.

Physical Education, Challenge, and Risk

One of the things I find most concerning is that many kids simply do not have the basic physical foundation for simple, fundamental movements. What I observe on the playgrounds is that many five- and six-year-old kids don't know how to throw a ball, they don't have the agility, strength, coordination or courage to jump onto an object, like a bench, or a curb, or a tree stump. They cannot run efficiently, they lack strength, proprioception, and hand-eye coordination. They cannot hit the rim of a basketball hoop. To me, these issues are a huge failing. I believe that children are designed for movement. Children are constantly hurtling through space. Have you noticed the children never really walk from one place to the other? They run. The boys especially are constantly wrestling. If there's a tree, kids will climb it. Most kids are tagging and egging each other on and playing games that encourage movement.

I have been working on these skills with my son since he was a little baby. He started swim lessons at eight weeks old. Ever since he was just a toddler, I have been encouraging him to jump up onto stuff, to catch stuff, to throw stuff, to do anything and everything physical. I even have a little video when he was only learning to crawl, where I was encouraging him to crawl up a couple of steps from our living room to the dining room. We were both delighted when he succeeded. Pre-pandemic, Dov was doing swimming, rock climbing, jiu jitsu, and hip hop dance classes. I constantly challenged him and worked him out on the playground and around our CrossFit gym. I taught him to ride a bike, to play soccer and basketball.

By simply observing kids on the playgrounds, I see that many parents appear to have abdicated their responsibility to teach their kids these basic fundamental physical skills. So a long chapter (Chapter 20) in this book is dedicated to those lessons. How do you encourage your children to love moving their body? How do you encourage them to take pride in their physical achievements? How do you encourage their courage? How do you prepare them to move through life?

A note on competitiveness and safety. Not all children have the same temperament, nor the same tolerance for risk. Many children enjoy dosing themselves with little hits of fear, such as climbing up something that's a little too high, or riding their scooter down a hill a bit too fast. Conquering those fears is how they develop. There are also many children that simply are risk-averse, and want to play it safe. They do not want to take chances on the playground, such as going up the rock climbing wall, or going down the big slide, or engaging in some sort of obstacle course. Some children don't seem to have a competitive bone in their body. They do not feed off of competition with their peers; in fact they get discouraged and they withdraw from this type of challenge. Some kids have physical limitations. I fully understand this, and I know that it does not make sense to push past your child's comfort level or ability to the point where they are going to get frustrated, resentful and upset.

But physical limitations aside, I also believe that some of this is a nature vs. nurture question. Children may be averse to physical challenges and risk because parents simply have not encouraged them, or have not offered it as an option. Or, perhaps, they have been too coddled and insulated from challenge and risk altogether. How does your child react when they fall down and get a scrape, or if a ball hits them in the face? Are they afraid to fail? How resilient are they? How have you conditioned them to respond? If we begin to encourage our children early, then we will in fact help them develop the grit they need to move through life. After all, haven't we all eventually learned as adults, that, out there in the real world, it's risk and competition that are the engine of success?

Your Mileage May Vary

I don't expect everyone reading this book to agree with my approach. After all, I am just a parent who saw a need and took the opportunity to address it. As I said, I am not a professional educator, and I don't have any fancy education degrees. Some people reading this book might say: "This person is dilettante! He has no idea what he's talking about, and he cannot possibly understand my child." That's fine. I agree with you. I don't expect that my approach will work for everyone.

But I have worked with a significant enough sample of children, of all varying talents, risk profiles and abilities, and I have seen that children can often move from one state of mind to another quite fluidly. I've seen risk-averse children. Kids that did not believe in themselves on the playground, or in a particular activity. Children that didn't seem to want to compete in any way. And I have seen these kids develop to a point where they now embrace and even seek out challenges.

So it's up to you, whether you want to push your child or not. All of us parents want to be proud of our kids. We want to know that we did the best we could with them. That's what this book is really about.

1. BASIC MATH.

Adding and Subtracting Small Numbers

As I began homeschooling, I immediately recalled my own struggles with algebra. I remembered being very frustrated, sometimes in tears. It doesn't take much failure to discourage kids from enjoying math, and when you couple failure to learn with failure to teach, you've got a math death spiral. Do you really want your kid to say the proverbial "I'm not good at math", and have that mindset drive their future educational and career goals?

When I started math in earnest with Dov, I had a very clear goal: Build his confidence, and make him believe that he's the kid that's "really good at math".

In March, when our homeschool experiment began, Dov was already well on his way to adding small numbers. He had a good grasp of the numbers 0 - 10, and could add under 10 fairly quickly, using his fingers if necessary.

My first technique was to teach him to achieve larger sums, venturing beyond that formidable boundary of "10". 8 + 9, 7 + 6 and so on. The technique I used was rather simple. There's a point after which counting on your fingers is no longer possible. Past that point, it makes sense to simply draw and count some circles to represent the problem. For example, if you have 8 + 9, you can draw 8 circles, and then 9 more circles. Then you can count all of them together and get the answer. In order to do this, two things have to be in place: (1) your kid has to confidently recognize the numbers and (2) your kid has to be able to count, carefully and deliberately.

There are plenty of basic training tools for both of these things. What I did, and still do with some of the kids, is talk about numbers in a way that makes them familiar and comfortable. For example, we might discuss the number 7, and ask: "What can you think of in your life that has the number 7?" Well, we've obviously got 7 days of the week, 7 continents, 7 colors of the rainbow. Do this brainstorming exercise for all the basic numbers 1-10, and repeat and point out numbers to your kid daily.

Back to our circles. 8 + 9 would look like this:
OOOOOOOO and OOOOOOOOO

Here's of the best pieces of advice I've ever gotten: If something is constantly running through your head, like a difficult thought or task, the best way to get it OUT of your head is to write it down on paper. It's pretty magical, like an exorcism of sorts. By putting it on paper, your brain no longer has the responsibility to store that thought.

I believe that the Circles Method is the literal representation of the above advice. If you ask your kid, early on in their math learning: "What's 8+9?" they would probably freak out or shut down or simply shrug their shoulders. However, by getting it into a visual representation on paper, suddenly the problem is not so complex or scary as it seemed!

The same technique goes for subtraction of larger numbers - again, up to 20 or so, until drawing circles becomes impractical. Keep in mind that Circles Method is really the gateway to building your kid's confidence. After that, we are moving on to real adding and subtracting on paper. So if you were to say, "Brooklyn, what's 19 - 12?" the visual representation would look like this:

First, Brooklyn draws 19 circles:

OOOOOOOOOOOOOOOOOOO

Now, how many are we subtracting? 12. OK, so let's carefully cross out or black out 12 of the circles you just drew, one at a time, and then let's count how many are remaining.

~~OOOOOOOOOOOO~~OOOOOOO

I love this method because it's so simple and portable. Even if you don't have a pen and paper, you can use just about anything to achieve the same result. In fact, it can even be more fun and delightful. Twigs on the playground. Pebbles on the beach. Lego pieces. Grapes. Cheerios.

In a later chapter, I talk about using the card game Blackjack to teach Dov math in a similar way. This, and many other board games are useful tools to reinforce arithmetic. One of Dov's favorite games is Number Zingo, where you have to be able to quickly do basic counting and addition. It also tests response speed and focus, and it feels like a game, not like "doing math". It's very sneaky and effective. I would highly recommend it.

Adding Two- and Three- Digit Numbers, and Beyond

Once you feel that your kid has mastered the Circle Method, and has even begun to add numbers comfortably in her head, it's time to move on to a more practical method of adding larger numbers.

I began with the easier stuff, again in order to build Dov's confidence. For example, 44+33 or 11+27 don't require "carrying" a 1, which made it a very straightforward and logical extension of what Dov already knew how to do well. The key here is to teach the format of lining up the numbers properly in a vertical fashion. It's also important to pay careful attention to the sign. Is it a plus? Or minus? I used the example of buckling your seatbelt and checking your mirrors before you begin driving. You should never drive without doing those things first. Similarly, never begin a math problem without checking the sign, and properly lining up your numbers.

First I taught Dov how to convert a verbal problem, or one that's written horizontally, such as 44 + 33, into one that is easy to add on paper:

```
 44     11
+33    +27
____   ____
```

Once here, the basic arithmetic skills kick in, and your kid will know that 4 + 3 is 7, and therefore the answer is 77.

Moving to the next level of challenge, now we add numbers that require a "carry". For example, 27 + 27, or 18 + 9. The key here is to immediately turn the carry action into a game. In 27 + 27, 7 + 7 is 14, but "Oh no! There's only room for the 4, and the 1 can't fit! So we have to kick the 1 upstairs so that he can fit into the next column, and we can add him to those numbers." I began anthropomorphising numbers from the start, because it made them feel much more approachable, and made the math softer, kinder, and more fun.

Once your kid masters adding two, two-digit numbers, as well as a carry operation, you can start expanding to three and four digits. The mechanism is the same.

Subtracting Two- and Three- Digit Numbers, and Beyond

The idea is obviously very similar to the addition method above. However, I actually found the gameplay of subtraction more fun than addition. That's because I was able to come up with a fun, creative method to "borrow".

For example, if we are doing a problem like 54 - 38, again the first step is to convert it into the vertical format.

 54
-38
——

Now, the fun part - "The Knock".

The conversation goes something like this: "Well, let's start with the right-hand side, as always.

Quick Detour: Right vs. Left. Most five- to seven-year old kids can't quickly identify their right and left. This comes up all the time. The quickest way to determine which hand is a kid's dominant hand is to ask, "Which hand do you wipe your butt with?" Sure, you can ask which hand they eat or write with, but my suggestion is more fun and basically foolproof.

Back to 54 - 38. Let's see, we've got 4 minus 8. Can we do it? Uh-oh! No we cannot, because 8 is larger than 4, and we cannot subtract a larger number from a smaller one! (Imagine if you had 4 candies, and your friend said to you, 'Can I have 8 candies?' It can't be done since the number you have is smaller than the number he wants.) So, first, I knock on the table. "Who is it?" "Hey, 5, it's your neighbor, 4." "What do you want, 4?" "Well, listen, I hate to ask, but I've got this 8 here that I need to subtract, and I am simply too small to do it! Could I borrow a 1 from you?" "Sure, buddy." So, the 4 borrows a 1 from the 5, and now the little 4 becomes a mighty 14! (Make sure to reinforce how that works, and that the 4 doesn't become a 5, nor does it become a 41. These will be common mistakes your kid will make in the beginning.) Now, can we do 14 minus 8? Sure! Maybe we need to do Circle Method to make sure we don't make a mistake? What's the answer? 6. Great. Write that below the line, in the right column. So now we move on to the next column. Our 5 gave away a 1, remember, so it became a 4. What's 4 - 3? Easy, that's just 1. Write that below the line in the left column. So the answer is 16! It really helps to work on graph paper initially, or you can draw the columns showing how the numbers line up with each other. It's easy to expand this method to 3- and 4- digit numbers and beyond.

Adding and Subtracting More Than 2 Numbers

The next level of challenge here would be to add or subtract multiple numbers, such as:

44 + 33 + 28 + 47 + 102 + 21.

The mechanism remains the same. We tell the same stories about "not fitting" or "borrowing". The trick here is to teach your kid to stay really organized from the beginning. Writing sloppy numbers, not keeping to appropriate columns, getting signs confused will all be very demoralizing at this stage. Teach your kid to write neatly and deliberately. If the list of numbers to add/subtract is too overwhelming, teach them to break the problem up into manageable pieces.

Throwing so many numbers at your kid can be overwhelming to the point that they get discouraged, or attention span wanders, and they simply don't want to engage any more. The best way I found to fight this fatigue is to turn it all into a game. For example, if you have a bingo game at home, you can have your kid be the one to draw the numbers they'll eventually work with. Or you can simply write some numbers on post-it notes and have your kid draw several post-its out of a hat. You can also use the ages of the people you know. "How old is grandma? 71. OK, and how old am I? 38. Ok, so how much older is grandma?" Or, asked another way, "What's the difference between our ages?" And so on. Relating the numbers to real people, and then asking the questions makes this much more relevant and interesting for your kid. "How old is our entire family, combined?", or "What is the sum of all of our family's ages?"

Arithmetic Vocabulary - "Total, Sum, Difference"

I am not a fan of worksheets. I prefer applied math problems that kids can actually relate to, and ones that make kids think critically rather than just solve on autopilot. You'll see many of these lessons in the following chapter. I also really like word problems because they force kids to do some writing as well, which accomplishes two things: they practice penmanship, and they have to look at the data and draw conclusions. Much more useful for the real world.

To prepare them for arithmetic word problems, I teach the kids that any time they see "SUM" or "TOTAL", they should immediately think of addition or plus. Any time they see the word "DIFFERENCE", they should immediately think of subtraction.

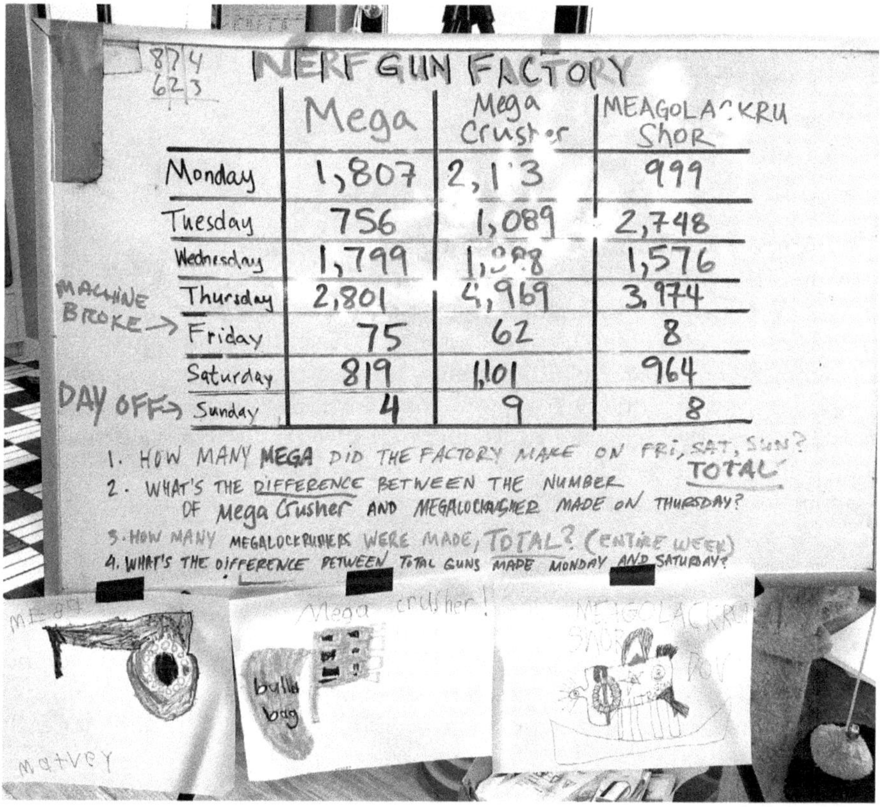

My word problems are always about things kids love, like doughnuts or Nerf guns, because it helps them immediately relate, and get their heads in the game. In the next chapter, you will see how I structure math lessons with real-world challenges. As an example, I had them draw their own Nerf guns, and name them. Not surprisingly, "mega" and "crusher" were the most popular ideas. Now I presented the production data for a Nerf gun factory. Then I asked them to interpret the data. Notice how the questions specifically use TOTAL and DIFFERENCE. The last question is sneaky because you have to first calculate the total, and then the difference.

1. How many Mega did the factory make on Friday, Saturday and Sunday, TOTAL?

2. What's the difference between the number of Mega Crusher and Megalockrusher (!) made on Thursday?

3. How many Megalockrusher were made, TOTAL (entire week)?

4. What's the difference between the TOTAL guns made on Monday and on Saturday?

Division

I found division to be a surprisingly easy concept to teach. My tools: playing cards and almonds. Let's take a sample problem, like 15 divided by 5. Now you just have to rephrase it as "I have 15 almonds, and 5 kids. How many almonds should each kid get so that all have the same amount?" Kids can immediately relate to this framing because they are very sensitive to making sure that nobody has more than anybody else. (Kids are natural communists?) I've actually had to put goldfish on a kitchen scale before to assure kids that everyone is getting the same amount. They would accept nothing less than empirical proof.

So what we do, is we lay out several face cards, and assign each a name, to make it even more relatable. Now we say, "How many almonds are we giving out? Ah, yes. 15!" So first we will count the almonds to make sure we have a pile of 15. Now, what we will do, is we will start giving one almond at a time to each "kid", until we run out of almonds. If each kid ends up with the same amount, then we know we did it right. And the amount each kid has is the answer.

You can repeat this same exercise with different numbers, but they should be a manageable amount. Don't make your kids count 138 almonds. 9 and 3, 16 and 4, 10 and 2… keep it simple and you'll get more reps to reinforce the concept. To supercharge this lesson, use M&M's or gummy bears instead of almonds, and tell your kid that if she does 10 problems correctly, the candy is hers at the end.

Multiplication

I think multiplication is the hardest to teach. But it's much easier if you do it on the heels of the division lesson, using the same tools. The first thing to convey to your kid is that when they see the "x" sign, or the words "multiply" or "times", they should immediately think "groups". For example, 5x3 is just 5 groups of 3, or 3 groups of 5. So then using your almonds, or coins, or Skittles, or whatever you have at hand, have the kid practice creating 3 groups of 5. Once done, count all the objects. That's pretty much all there is to it. After this introduction, it's just reps and reps and reps. Practice, practice, practice.

Once your kid feels comfortable with this concept, you can move on to larger numbers. I found it very effective to teach larger numbers using 10's. For example, when you multiply any number by 10, you simply add a zero.

That's easy enough to understand. 1x10? 10. 2x10? 20. And so on. Your kids will get this right away because they are hardwired to look for patterns. You'll be overjoyed to see their delight at immediately grasping this pattern. Now, once they've got it, you can go back and remind them that 2x10 is just 2, 10 times. Or 10 groups of 2. So what about 2x9? Seems hard, but it's not. Why? Because you just figured out what 2x10 is, you know that's 20. So 2x9 is just one less group of 2 than 2x10. If 2x10 is 20, then 20 - 2 is what? Right. 18. As your kid gets more comfortable with arithmetic, and can do problems like 120 + 12, then a multiplication problem like 12x11 is not scary at all. Since 12x10 is 120 (we just add the zero), then 12x11 is just one more 12 than that, so what's 120 + 12? 132. Easy.

A Different Approach: Multiplication and Area Using Magna-Tiles®

Multiplication can be intimidating, but you can make it friendly by using an approach and a tool that kids can relate to. Almost all kids have - and love - their set of Magna-Tiles®. Use the square-shaped Magna-Tiles® to help kids quickly visualize the "groups" concept. What is 5x6? Well, it's just five groups of six, or six groups of five. With the magnetic squares, it's quick and fun for kids to form these groups. My kids definitely found Magna-Tiles® math much more fun and engaging than doing it on paper. I suppose the only thing that would be even better is if I dumped a huge bag of lollipops on the table.

Once you get enough practice making Magna-Tiles® groups, you can move on to calculating area. If you form a 2x2 square using the magnetic squares, it's very easy to prove that the area of this square is in fact, four. You can calculate it different ways: (1) It's two groups of two, which is four. (2) You can individually count all the squares in front of you. Still four. Now you can prove to your kid that 2x2 is indeed four. From here, expand to larger squares, 3x3, 5x5 and so on. Then move on to rectangles. For a higher level challenge, move on to calculating the area of a triangle. A typical Magna-Tiles® set has a number of right triangle pieces that are exactly half the size of a square. If you join two of these right triangles together, it will form a square. You can visually prove to your kid that one of these right triangles is exactly half of a square. One they are convinced of this, you can demonstrate that the area of a this right triangle is just the two non-diagonal sides multiplied together, then divided by two. Why divided by two? Well, remember, the triangle is clearly just half of the square.

"Math Magic" - Getting Kids to Do Math in Their Heads

There's a silly old "magic trick" I learned a long time ago. It's an obvious way of manipulating numbers that makes it appear as if you can "read" someone's mind. The real trick here is that young kids find it very impressive, and if you can get them hooked, you might actually trick them into doing arithmetic in their heads!

The trick goes like this: The Math Magician asks someone to think of a number in their head between 1 and 10. (You might have them write it down, and/or discreetly show it to others, in case they might forget later. Obviously this could happen with really young kids.)

Now, the Magician takes the number-picker through a series of basic arithmetic moves.

> "Ok, take the number you just thought of and add 2. Now subtract 1. Now add 6. Now subtract 4. Now subtract 2. Now add 3. Now add 4. Now subtract 5. Now subtract your ORIGINAL number."

Don't overdo it, because really young kids will either lose track, or lose interest, or both. Now, you pretend to concentrate very hard, and you might even put your hand on the number-picker's head, as if stealing their thoughts. After a moment's hesitation for suspense, and with the flair and pride of a professional magician, you triumphantly announce that the number NOW in the person's head is 3!

Of course, the trick here is that once you "subtract your original number", you're just looking at the end result of all your arithmetic. Slightly older kids will figure this out, but this game is designed to trick young kids into doing basic math in their heads. And if you inspire them properly, they too can have a turn at being the Math Magician and reading other peoples' minds.

I've used this game at a magic show for the kids. It's even more fun when you've got a cape and a top hat and you introduce this as one of your "world famous" acts. At that point, once you offer the kids to wear the cape and top hat, they will definitely take you up on it.

This game is scalable, because you can graduate to larger numbers, and you can even slyly start to do more complicated arithmetic on the whiteboard. I begin to represent the "original number" as X, starting to plant the seeds for algebra. Kids may go through a few iterations with you before they realize they're actually just doing math. Suckers.

2. APPLYING MATH TO REAL WORLD CHALLENGES.

Build the Fastest Car

Eventually, I noticed that Dov was getting pretty bored with the usual arithmetic lessons. Once he learned how to add and subtract fairly large numbers, it made sense to find a way to apply his new knowledge. I devised several lessons on topics that I knew he would enjoy, such as "build the fastest car" or "mission to mars" or "build the fastest airplane". The premise was that he'd have to make a set of decisions to achieve the objective, and work with some constraints.

To build the fastest car, he would have $1,000 to spend on purchasing several components. He would start with a shell of a car, and have to purchase an engine, tires, an interior and brakes. Optionally he could also buy a spoiler and rims. Each component had several levels of "quality", from basic to luxury, or as he called it, from "default" to "mythic". Choosing components required a lot of arithmetic, as well as some basic multiplication (since you have to get four tires, etc). Each component came with a certain improvement speed.

The point of the exercise was not necessarily to get him to choose the optimal combination of components based on price and speed - honestly, since I made these up on the fly, even I couldn't do it without a spreadsheet. The point was to get him to think critically and put his math skills to good use. The nice thing about this lesson is that you can scale it to your kid's current math ability. For a total beginner, you can use really small and simple numbers (e.g. $10 budget, only a couple of decision points and basic prices like $1 or $2.)

I expanded this math lesson structure to include "Mission to Mars" and "Build the Fastest Airplane". Mars had to more with division, calculating distances, figuring out the amount of fuel required. Airplane worked with even larger numbers than Car, with a budget of $1,000,000. The idea there was to keep building his confidence working with large numbers that are in the tens and hundreds of thousands.

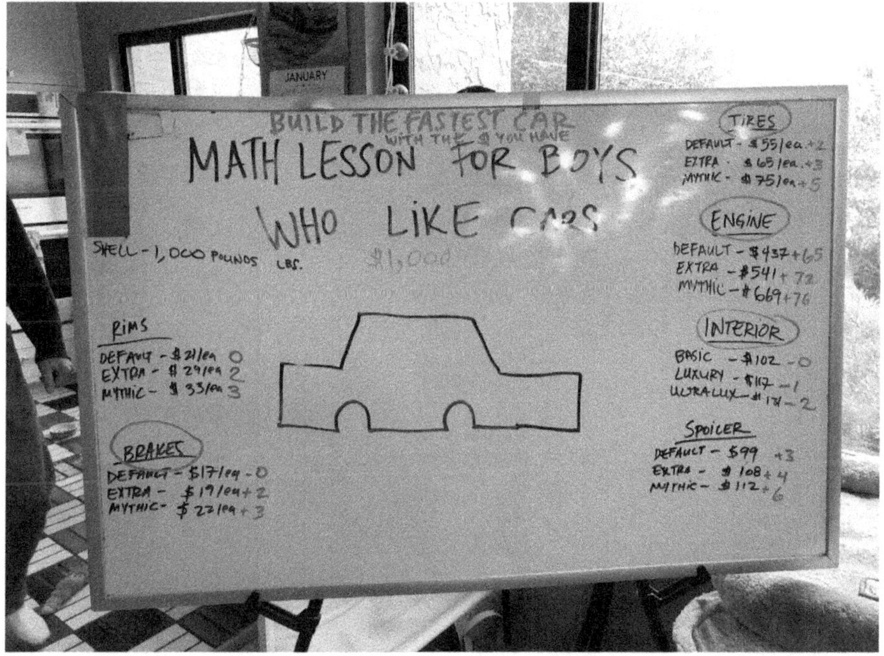

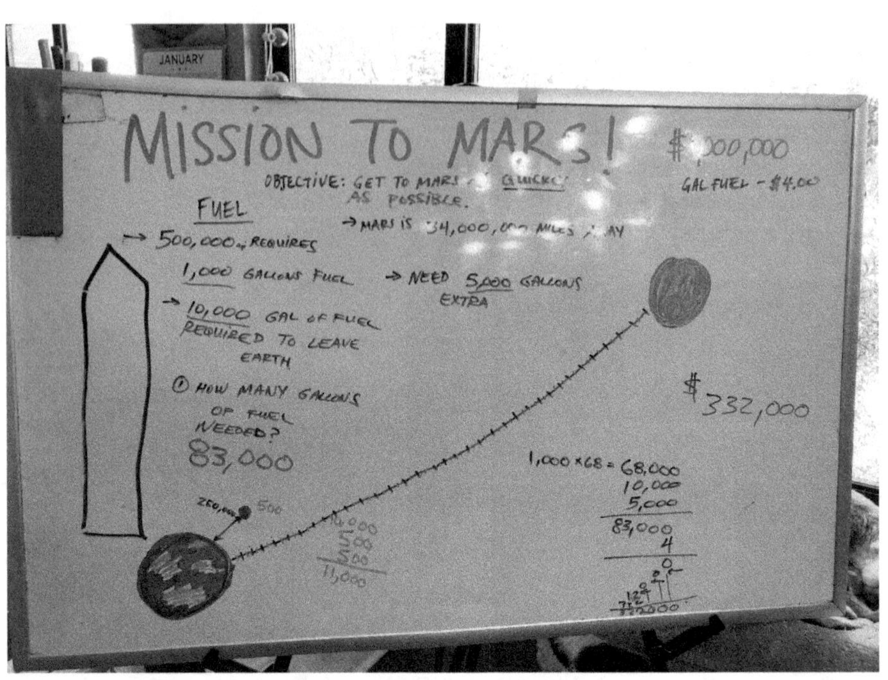

MISSION TO MARS!
OBJECTIVE: GET TO MARS
AS POSSIBLE.
GAL FUEL - $4.00
FUEL
→ 500,000 REQUIRES
1,000 GALLONS FUEL
→ NEED 5,000 GALLONS EXTRA
→ 10,000 GAL OF FUEL REQUIRED TO LEAVE EARTH
① HOW MANY GALLONS OF FUEL NEEDED?
83,000
$332,000
1,000 × 68 = 68,000
10,000
5,000
83,000
4

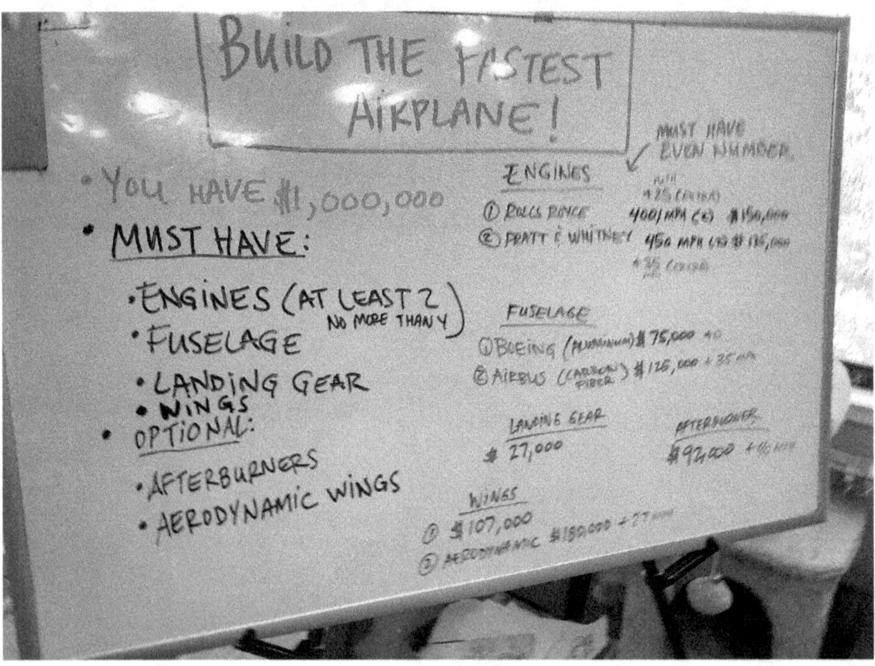

BUILD THE FASTEST AIRPLANE!
• YOU HAVE $1,000,000
• MUST HAVE:
• ENGINES (AT LEAST 2 NO MORE THAN 4)
• FUSELAGE
• LANDING GEAR
• WINGS
• OPTIONAL:
• AFTERBURNERS
• AERODYNAMIC WINGS
ENGINES
MUST HAVE EVEN NUMBER
① ROLLS ROYCE 400 MPH
② PRATT & WHITNEY 450 MPH
FUSELAGE
① BOEING (ALUMINUM) $75,000
② AIRBUS (CARBON FIBER) $125,000
LANDING GEAR
$27,000
AFTERBURNER
$92,000
WINGS
① $107,000
② AERODYNAMIC $180,000

Barbell Math

I am passionate about CrossFit. This sport challenges you mentally as well as physically, and a common mental challenge is doing "barbell arithmetic" as you add and strip plates from the bar during workouts.

I think this is a perfect applied math challenge for kids as well. The beauty of "barbell math" is that it's such a flexible tool to quickly generate a large number of math problems. The easiest way to begin is to draw a stick figure holding a barbell. Assign a weight to the bar, and a weight to one plate on each side. The barbell should always be balanced; one side cannot be heavier than the other. Ask your kid to do basic arithmetic and add up the bar and the two weights on each side.

Now you can start adding weights to create more challenge, and also you can only show the values for the weights on one side. This is more challenging because now your kid has to fill in the blanks and remember that the two sides must be equal.

Next level is to turn this into a subtraction problem, where you give the TOTAL weight of the barbell, and then ask the kid to deduce how much bar itself weighs if given all the weights of the plates.

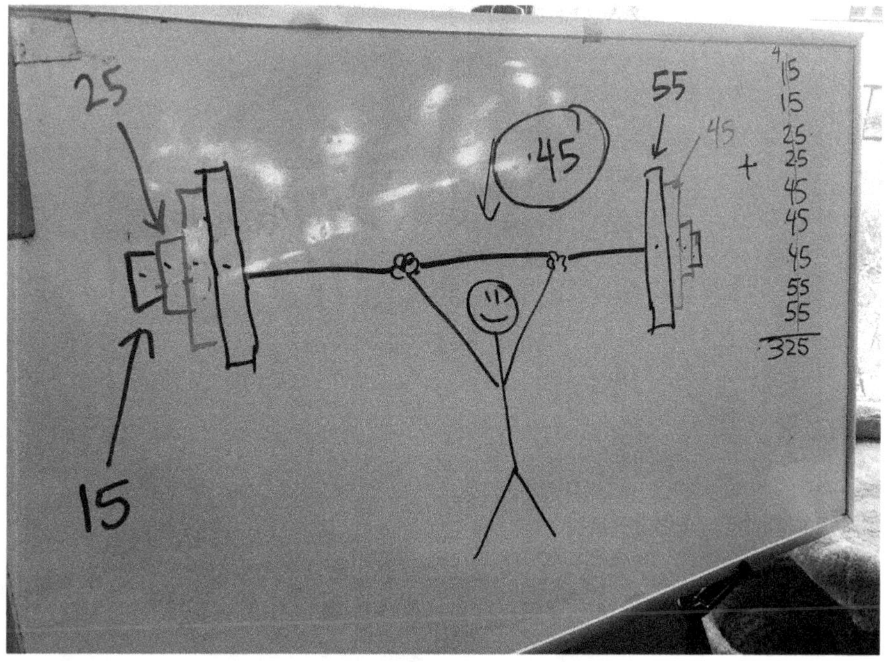

The Time Machine

A great way to get kids comfortable doing arithmetic with three- and four- digit numbers - hundreds and thousands - is to use the example of a Time Machine. First, I had them settle down and draw their time machines, which was a fun way to get them engaged and warmed up for the lesson. Now we put a timeline on the whiteboard, and give examples of some trips taken by the time traveler. For example, we travel from the "Present" 2021 into the "Future" 2276. How many years forward did we travel? Here I introduce the concept of "difference". Any time you see the word "difference" in math, you should think subtraction. Should we subtract the big number from the small? Or the small from the big?

You can use this model to have them make several trips backwards and forwards in time, each time practicing setting up and solving a subtraction problem. By making the subject of the problem years instead of just random large numbers, it gives more context and makes the lesson less intimidating.

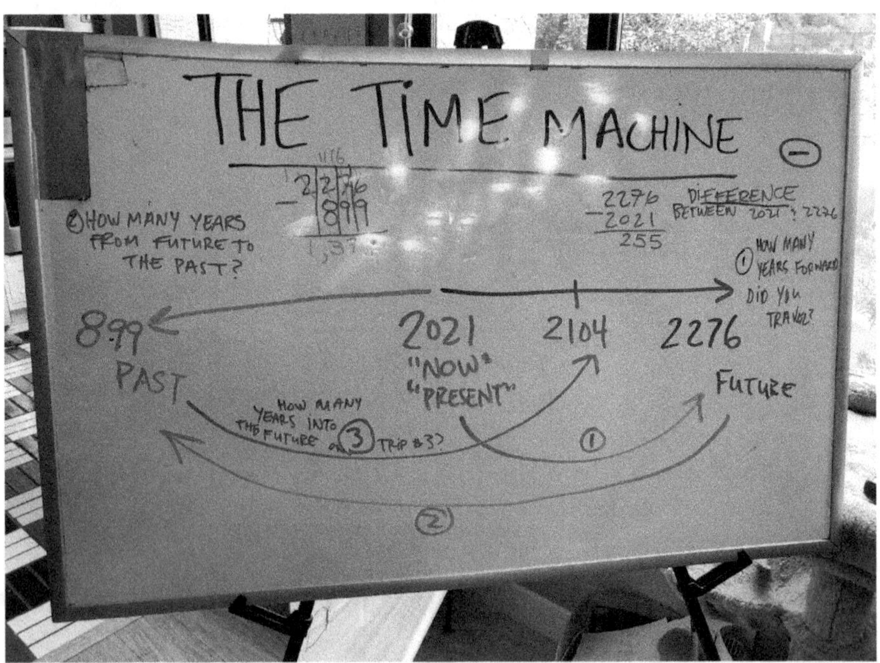

"Spreadsheets"

I really like compound exercises: assignments that challenge the kids to do more than one thing well. For example, here we built a spreadsheet for a pizza restaurant, showing how many types of each pizza were sold on each day of the week. This really hits several major points: (1) good penmanship (2) staying organized (3) reviewing the days of the week (4) practicing spelling (5) understanding how to use a table or grid (6) actually doing the arithmetic (7) allowing to push further for more challenging questions.

It was not easy for some kids to neatly fit all the letters into the rectangles on the grid, especially for long words like "Wednesday" and "Parmesan Cheese". I gave the kids an empty grid to begin with, and they had to fill it in by following along with the whiteboard. One trick I used was having them trade different color gel pens with one another for each pizza type. It made the assignment more fun, solved several "but-I-wanted-the-blue!" conflicts, and also helped them stay organized by essentially color coding their tables.

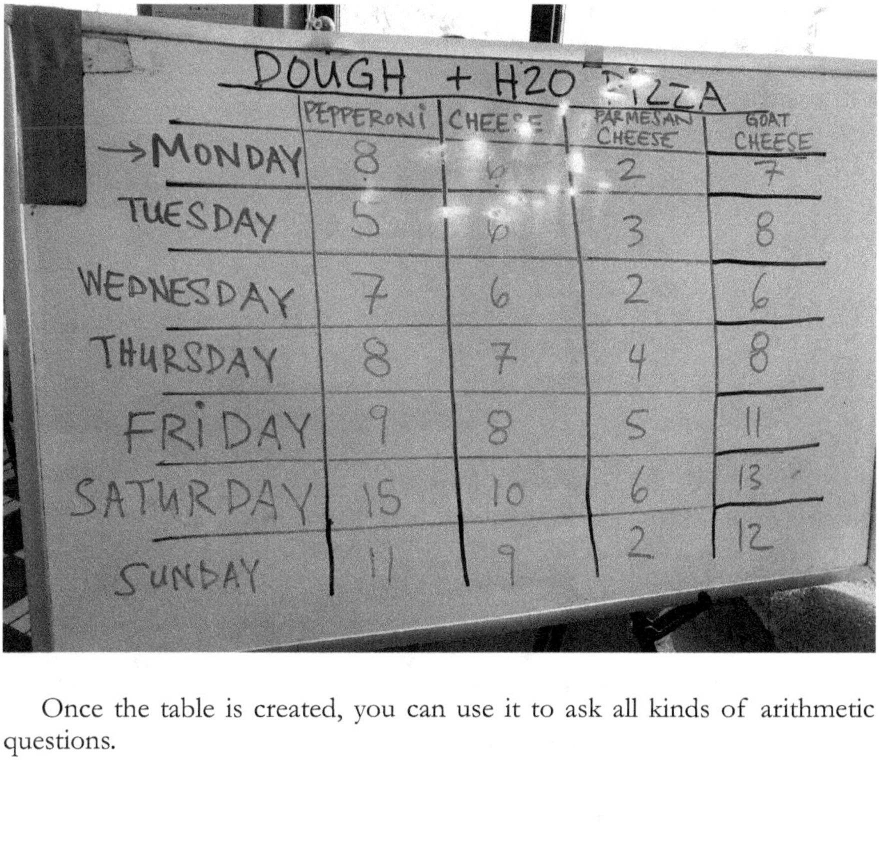

DOUGH + H2O PIZZA

	PEPPERONI	CHEE	PARMESAN CHEESE	GOAT CHEESE
→MONDAY	8	6	2	7
TUESDAY	5	6	3	8
WEDNESDAY	7	6	2	6
THURSDAY	8	7	4	8
FRIDAY	9	8	5	11
SATURDAY	15	10	6	13
SUNDAY	11	9	2	12

Once the table is created, you can use it to ask all kinds of arithmetic questions.

Level 1: "How many Cheese pizzas were sold on Monday?"
Level 2: "How many total pizzas were sold on Friday?"
Level 3: "Which is the most popular pizza? Which is the busiest day?"

As with pretty much any assignment in this book, you can always scale up the level of difficulty. For my advanced math class, I created a more challenging version called the Donut Factory. Of course I let the kids come up with the donut types, which they enjoyed immensely. The numbers were larger and so required much more challenging arithmetic. The questions got more difficult as well, such as "How many more chocolate sprinkle donuts were made than frosting donuts?"

You can also throw in some wrinkles that encourage critical thinking. For example, on Thursday the number of donuts made were much lower than all other weekdays. On Saturday and Sunday as well, fewer donuts were made. I asked the kids to come up with some possible explanations for why this might be the case.

You can use this concept to give pretty much any example. I created a later lesson where we compared delivery companies, UPS, FedEx, DHL and USPS. I scaled up the difficulty and had them work with larger numbers. I love this approach because it's not *really* about the arithmetic. What's really critical here is the setup - making sure that your kid stays organized and focused, maintaining place value, and not getting discouraged despite the intimidating big numbers. The rest is just process.

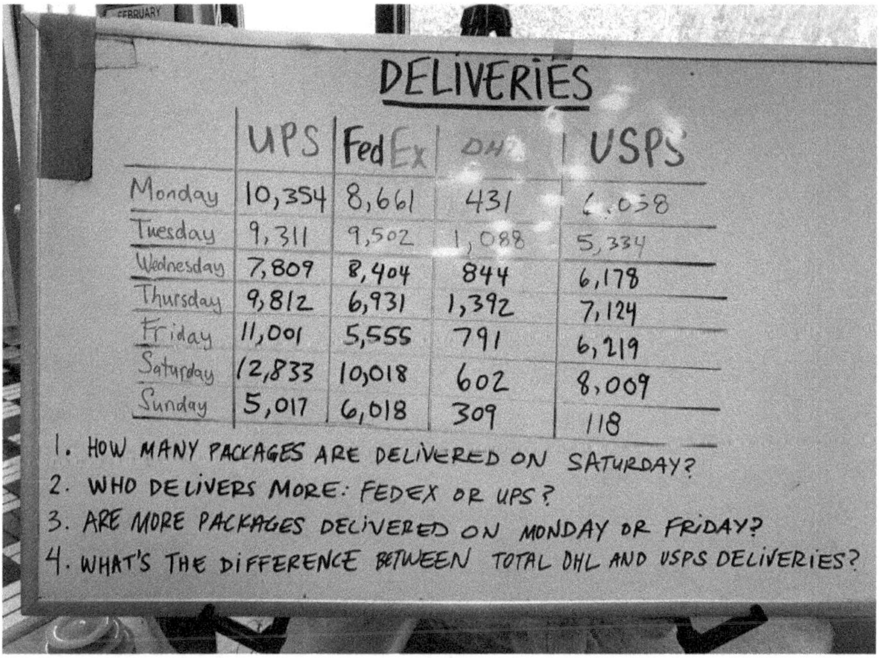

DELIVERIES

	UPS	FedEx	DH	USPS
Monday	10,354	8,661	431	6,038
Tuesday	9,311	9,502	1,088	5,334
Wednesday	7,809	8,404	844	6,178
Thursday	9,812	6,931	1,392	7,124
Friday	11,001	5,555	791	6,219
Saturday	12,833	10,018	602	8,009
Sunday	5,017	6,018	309	118

1. HOW MANY PACKAGES ARE DELIVERED ON SATURDAY?
2. WHO DELIVERS MORE: FEDEX OR UPS?
3. ARE MORE PACKAGES DELIVERED ON MONDAY OR FRIDAY?
4. WHAT'S THE DIFFERENCE BETWEEN TOTAL DHL AND USPS DELIVERIES?

3. THE ALPHABET. VOWELS, CONSONANTS, AND SYLLABLES.

The foundation for reading lies in understanding these fundamental concepts. It turns out that by the age of 5, most children know the alphabet only in song. ABCDEFG is pretty good, then it can turn into HIJKNMNOPURFTUmmmm….andZ. If your child doesn't know the alphabet, you have to begin there. There's no magic bullet.

I would recommend dedicating each day to a new letter. Do everything you can reinforce the letter.

Write the letter and talk about what the letter resembles. Draw it together so your kid can visualize it. Here are some of my suggestions:

"A" looks vaguely like a house, or maybe an open ladder
"B" looks like a fat hippopotamus
"C" looks like the link of a chain that was slightly pulled apart by a strongman
"D" looks like a sideways smile
"E" looks like a sideways comb
"F" looks like a squirt gun (the little part of the F is the trigger, it's shooting downward)
"G" looks like a sideways rainbow; the bottom is the leprechaun's tophat upside down
"H" looks like a pull-up bar
"I" looks like a birthday candle
"J" looks like a fish hook
"K" looks like two kids that got into a fight and are standing back to back, with the one on the right bending over and crying

"L" looks like a hockey stick
"M" looks like the Golden Gate Bridge
"N" looks like lightning
"O" looks like a donut
"P" looks like a baseball cap
"Q" looks like a lasso (cowboy's rope)
"R" looks like an upside-down bunny
"S" looks like a snake
"T" looks like a swingset on a playground
"U" looks like a cup
"V" looks like the V sign you make w/ your middle and index fingers, or a unicorn's horn that fell off.
"W" looks like a person jumping onto a trampoline, bouncing up, then hitting the ceiling, bouncing down, then hitting another trampoline and bouncing up again. Get creative. The more ridiculous and unusual the comparison, the better they will remember the shape of the letter.
"X" looks like "X marks the spot" on pirate treasure map
"Y" looks like a slingshot
"Z" looks like swordsman making three slashes (Google Zorro)

Come up with simple, familiar words that start with each letter. Make it into a game where your kid has to help you brainstorm the words. Maybe you can make it into a "competition" to see who can brainstorm more words. Help them along and give ample hints so they don't get frustrated. Make intentional mistakes that your kid will find funny to break up "education" with a little comic relief. (More on the beauty of intentional mistakes later).

Constantly reinforce the words and letters. Use every opportunity: driving, walking, watching TV, shopping for groceries. Any time you spot a letter or a useful example, stop your kid and point it out.

Vowels

The simplest way to explain vowels is to demonstrate that they are long sounds we can sustain with our mouths open. AAAAAA….. EEEEEEE….. IIIIIII….. OOOOOO….. UUUUUUUU. Focus on the shape of the mouth and take the opportunity to make ridiculous noises with your kid. The more ridiculous the better. Give examples:

AAAAAA is the sound you make when you go to the doctor and they examine your throat. Or the sound you make when you are terrified in a haunted house.

EEEEEE is the sound a creaky door makes.

IIIIIIIIIIIIII could be the sound of someone trying to answer a question and getting stuck or confused… "IIIIIIIIIIIIiiiiii forgot."

OOOOOOO is obviously the sound of a ghost, or maybe the sound kids make when they know another kid is about to get in trouble.

UUUUUUUUUUU is more of a guttural sound that someone might make if their stomach hurts from bad food or from getting hit with a ball.

Consonants

All the letters in the alphabet that are NOT vowels. Right? Consonants are all the letters with which you cannot make a sustained sound with your mouth open. Do lots of demonstrations and make silly, strained faces trying to squeeze a sustained sound out of a "K" or a "T" or a "W". Embrace the opportunity to make ridiculous shapes with your mouth and be goofy with your kid!

Syllables

Start putting vowels and consonants together. One game we came up with was to imagine what kind of creature would say ZA, ZE, ZI, ZO, ZU. Maybe an alien? WA, WE, WI, WO, WU - maybe a magician? (Extra emphasis on the "WA!") And so on.

Usually kids become familiar with the letters in their name more quickly than any others. Use that to your advantage and break down their name and other familiar names (yours, your partner's, grandparents', friends' and so on) into syllables. How many syllables are in the name Jackson? JACK-SON. Two! What about Brooklyn? BROOK-LYN. Also two!

I love the improv game Zip-Zap-Zop (see Chapter 9 on Improv Games). A great way to infuse some energy into your lesson while still learning syllables!

4. PUNCTUATION.

Basic Punctuation

For kids who are still spelling phonetically and getting comfortable with letters, punctuation may seem like jumping a bit too far ahead. I disagree. I feel like giving kids the full landscape of the written signs and symbols in their environment will give them a leg up.

I think it's effective to connect punctuation to emotion. The exercise is this: Draw a simple happy face on the whiteboard, and ask your kid to give her opinion on how that person is feeling. Now make a basic change: the smile becomes a frown. How does the person feel now? Now change the frown back to a smile, and add eyebrows, slanting downward. This gives the effect of making the face mischievous, scheming, even evil-looking. The point of this exercise is to illustrate that making a few simple marks can entirely change the way we perceive something. This becomes a perfect segue to talking about punctuation marks. Write a simple "YES." on the board, and read it as such, with a flat, neutral tone that the period suggests. Now, add a line and change the period to an exclamation mark. How do we pronounce the word now? Emphatically, of course! What about if we add two more exclamation marks? Let the kid have fun with this, yelling and getting louder each time. Now change to a question mark. Now change to ?!?!?. Play with the emotions of incredulity and shock. Experiment with these changes as long as your kid stays engaged, and reconnect it back to the "happy face / sad face" work that you did to open the lesson. Play with modifying other words and phrases that your kid can relate to: "I'm hungry. I'm hungry! I'm hungry? I'm hungry!!!"

Now, let's address the comma. The simplest way to boil down the comma's purpose, is to explain it as a "pause", and a good way to separate a list of things. "My favorite toys are: a truck, [pause] Star Wars Legos, [pause] and a pogo stick." Or: "I went to the pool this morning, and then I stopped by at the grocery store." I wouldn't get into too much more detail than this.

Apostrophe

The comma is also a great segue to the apostrophe. "Apostrophe" is a hard word for kids to read and pronounce, but it's also kind of fun. Instead of trying to force it by rote memorization, I thought of two "helper" words that are sort of distant cousins in terms of their pronunciation and structure. IMPOSTOR is a similar-sounding word, and also a really fun word to play with. I gave the kids the definition of impostor, and then pretended to be one of the kids, having a fake dialogue, accusing myself of being an impostor. Remember, if you make it into a game, they will remember it forever. I also played with the word CATASTROPHE, again a sort of cousin to apostrophe. I explained the definition and played with some imagined examples of catastrophes (many of which involved a messy playroom or kitchen, so the kid could really relate). I also thought it was particularly funny that CATastrophe has the word "cat" in it. I asked the kids to imagine other versions of the word, replacing CAT with other three-letter animals. Dogastrophe. Pigastrophe. Cowastrophe. The kids immediately came up with other fun ideas like Snakeastrophe, Peanutbutterastrophe and Astropheastrophe. Now that they had some fun, and got comfortable with the word structure, I steered the conversation back to apostrophe. I explained that it's commonly used to show the possessive form of something, for example "Lucie's toys", or "Eric's bike". I then wrote several phrases on the board and asked the kids to correct my mistakes. Several were written correctly, but in some I left out the apostrophe, for example "Jenny skateboard" and "Timmy sandwich". The kids were very quick to spot the missing "apostrophe S".

Punctuation in Math

Another great segue from punctuation is over to the math side of things. Turns out that the period and comma, and even the exclamation mark are all used in math as well. It's a great opportunity to talk to kids about place value, decimals, and even factorial if they've already begun to understand multiplication.

I did a very basic exercise where I steadily built numbers longer and longer, and asked kids to read each step.

For example:

8
88
888
8,888
88,888
888,888
8,888,888
88,888,888
888,888,888
8,888,888,888

Kids love to see patterns, and this one also becomes almost a tongue twister if you do it long enough. Explaining that the comma separates every three digits, so once you've got a four digit number, a comma is necessary. You can reinforce the concept with a mnemonic - if you see one comma, you're talking thousands. Two commas - millions. Three commas - billions. If you can get your kid to correctly identify numbers up to a billion, that's a huge win at this age.

To explain decimals, I used currency. I showed the kids a grocery store receipt and asked them to notice that pretty much every entry had two numbers after the period. Apples: $2.72; Bananas: $4.66 and so on. I explained that any numbers after the period are part of a dollar, not a whole dollar. Anything less than 100 cents would end up on the right side of the period.

Finally, the factorial is almost like a matryoshka, a Russian nesting doll. The exclamation mark signifies that inside this number, a whole string of numbers are waiting to be multiplied. 5! would be 5x4x3x2x1. Kids found it quite entertaining that several numbers would be "hiding" inside, and the exclamation mark was the signal to unpack them. Now, there's no question that factorials are a way advanced concept for a 1st grader. But I don't believe in wasting an opportunity to connect some dots or plant seeds that will pay off later. I hope by now you can see my approach: just look a little harder, you'll notice that everything is connected.

5. POSSIBILITY AND PROBABILITY.

These concepts were at the top of my list of useful, real-world knowledge. The ability to understand the difference between these ideas, as well as the language and tools of probability, seemed very necessary in everyday life. Teaching probability is also surprisingly easy, since we have lots of familiar games of chance at our fingertips. Moreover, once your kids become familiar with these tools, they can use them effectively to solve conflicts.

Quick Detour: It's important to resolve conflicts between kids quickly and effectively. Conflicts clog up the flow of ideas and halt the momentum of a lesson. Kids find opportunities to fight over everything: Who goes first. Who gets the red marker. She got more. I got less. It's exhausting if you constantly have to be the referee. I taught my kids early on that they already have a toolbox to help solve conflicts on their own. The easiest way? Rock, paper, scissors. Two out of three. Winner takes it. Alternatives? Flip a coin. Roll a die (highest roll wins).

Back to probability. I chose the following tools for the job: (1) deck of cards (2) dice (3) coin (4) colored ping pong balls. Some time ago I taught Blackjack to Dov, as a way of encouraging him to do simple addition in his head. I noticed that he was really excited by the dopamine hit of "the next card", and so I figured that probability games would be just as thrilling.

Let's begin with a coin, the simplest of all probability tools.

Explain that a coin only has two sides: head and tails. If you flip the coin, it will inevitably land on one side or the other. How many possibilities are there when you flip a coin? That's right, only two. And one of them

MUST come true. (Some precocious children may observe that a coin could land on its edge, and so you'll have to explain that this is so unlikely as to be *nearly* impossible). Since the coin only has two sides, the probability / chance / likelihood of each is exactly the same. This is also a great time to explain that EACH time you flip a coin, the probability resets. You can start slowly introducing language like "There are two possibilities, heads and tails, and only one of them will happen when you flip. So, the chance of the coin coming up heads is one out of two. The chance of tails is also one out of two. One result out of two possible results.

Now, introduce a six-sided die.

Ask the child to explain how the possibilities on a die are different from the coin. That's right: the die has six sides, each with its own unique number, one through six, and each of those numbers is equally likely to come up. Therefore, since there are six sides, there are six possibilities. Remember the coin? It only has two sides, and so only two possibilities. What is the probability / chance / likelihood that you will roll a three on the die? Well, how many three's are there? That's right, only one. And out of six possible numbers. So that means the chance you will roll a three on a die is one out of six. In fact, the chance of rolling ANY number on a die is one out of six.

Now, is the probability of rolling a three (or any other number) on a die higher than flipping tails on a coin? Or lower? Your child may struggle with this question, which is great. If this is in fact their first introduction to probability, there's no reason to think they will understand this intuitively. Now it's time to give a real-world example that any kid can understand.

"Let's say we are at a birthday party, and there's a piñata. There are six kids at the party, and each will have a chance to swing at the piñata and break it open. Let's say all the kids are equally strong. What is the chance that any one of the kids will be the one to break it? Yep, it's one out of six. One of those kids will break it open, but we don't know which one. Now, let's say it's your birthday your parents tell you that you get to break the piñata all by yourself. Now, is there any chance that someone else will break it? Absolutely not. It will definitely be you (it might take you a lot of swings and you might get tired, and your friends will kind of hate you, but it'll be worth it, right?) Which birthday party would you rather be at? Most kids should selfishly say that they'd prefer to be the only one swinging. Well then, what if your best friend convinces you that they also should have a turn to swing. So now instead of just you, it's you and your best friend. Which situation do you prefer now: You and your BFF, or you and five other kids? Right. With just you and you friend, the chance that either of you will break it open is one out of two, just like the coin. Two possibilities - either he or you. Heads or tails.

Let's pull out the deck of cards.

How many cards are in a deck? 52. There are 52 possibilities in that deck, all equally likely. The chance of pulling out any card is one out of 52. The Queen of Spades? One out of 52. The 10 of Clubs? One out of 52. The Three of Hearts? One out of 52. You can also explore the probabilities of pulling out colors - red or black. Hey! That's just like the coin! Or suits, Hearts, Clubs, Spades, Diamonds. Now there are four possibilities. If you want to get more advanced, you can now explain that the chance of pulling out a Spade is 13 out of 52, and same with all other suits.

13 out of 52 is the same as one out of four. If you want to push a level further, ask the question: "Let's say I want to pull out the Ace of Spades. What's my probability of doing that? That's right, one out of 52." Now pull a card. It's not the Ace of Spades. Now ask: "What's my probability of pulling the Ace now?" Your child might parrot: one out of 52. Great. Now explain, "Hang on, we already pulled a card, and it wasn't the Ace of Spades. There are how many cards left in the deck that we haven't seen? Aha! Only 51 cards left now. So the probability of pulling out the Ace of Spades now is one out of 51." And so on. As we keep pulling and seeing

more cards, our probability / chance / likelihood of pulling out the Ace of Spades keeps getting higher, since there are now fewer possibilities to pull out another card.

Put some colored ping pong balls into a hat: let's say five orange and five blue. Put a blindfold on your child. Now it's fun and it becomes a game. The sillier the blindfold the better. (There are some totally ridiculous animal and silly face blindfolds on Amazon).

Tell them to reach into the hat. Ask: "What's the probability that you pull out a blue ball?" That's right, five out of 10. Now go through the exercise of increasing/reducing the number of balls of each color.

It's now time for the Pirate Challenge.

Explain that the kid has been kidnapped by bloodthirsty pirates. These pirates are ruthless and will force most of their captives to walk the plank. I suggest having some rope or ribbon ready to actually tie your kid's hands behind her back. Also, cardboard from an Amazon box works great as a makeshift plank. Now explain that these pirates are feeling generous, and they give the kid some options of games of chance to play to try to save her life. She can choose from say, (1) flip a coin and get Tails (2) Pull out an orange ball from a hat with one orange ball and two blue balls (3) Pull a spade out of a deck of cards. If she can get lucky, they will spare her life. If not, she walks the plank. She has to decide, which game would she rather play to try to save her life? The important thing here is to focus on "chances to lose" or "chances to win". For example, with the coin, she has ONE chance to win and ONE chance to lose. With the balls, it's ONE chance to win and TWO chances to lose. And with the cards, it's ONE chance to win and THREE chances to lose. By walking her through it in this language, it should become clear which is the most advantageous option. Even if she picks wrong, it doesn't matter. Put on your best pirate accent and make her walk the plank if she loses, with a big "SPLOOOSH!" at the end for emphasis. Also, don't forget to mention the sharks.

Fractions

The next level up is to transition those probabilities into talking about fractions. Since you've already been writing them on the board, it's a logical next step to talk about the Numerator and Denominator. These are both big, difficult words, which makes them fun to play with. I started easy, just explaining that as we were showing the probabilities, we happened to write all these numbers. In any given probability, say your deck of cards, one number is above the line, and one below. With my kids, I actually had them act out being a numerator and denominator, by having one kid climb up on the table, and the other kid climb under. The table is the line, the kid on top is the numerator, the kid on bottom the denominator. As kids struggle to pronounce these words, "Demonitator" "Nurembater" etc., you should embrace this and play with the idea. Get goofy, get silly, make up weird anagrams and try to pronounce them. Make intentional mistakes (as you will see, intentional mistakes are an invaluable teaching tool).

Go back to your deck of cards and start to give different examples:

What's the probability of pulling out a spade? 13/52. 13 is the numerator, and 52 is the denominator.

What's the probability of pulling out a red card? Well there are 26 red cards and 52 total cards so it's 26/52. Keep reinforcing the words numerator and denominator. Keep embracing the tongue-twisting mistakes!

You begin to change the denominator to take it to the next level. This will eventually get your kid to start thinking a bit more deeply.

What if we take a full deck of cards (52) and try to pull out a Spade? What's our probability/chance of getting that? Well, of course it's 13/52. OK, let's try it! Oh, we pulled out the Four of Diamonds. OK, now what's our probability of pulling out a spade on the next attempt? This is where it gets fun of course, because now the denominator changes to 51 since one card is already gone from the deck. The numerator stays the same since all the spades are still there. So it's 13/51! And so on. Keep repeating with different examples.

A deck of cards is a magical teaching tool, because it holds the promise of the "next card". I think kids are by nature little gamblers and enjoy the dopamine hits. Blackjack helped Dov to learn to add in his head.

Quick Digression - Teaching Math With Blackjack

To that point, I found that Blackjack is a perfect tool to teach basic arithmetic. It's a very easy card game to explain to a kid, and since they love the little dopamine hit of the "next card", they forget that they're actually having to do math problems in their head to figure out if they want to stay or hit. My son absolutely loved this (I suppose I should be a little concerned about his gambling tendencies), and it made him jump ahead quite a bit in his ability to do basic math in his head.

Possible vs. Impossible

There's an opportunity here to really hammer home these two opposite words. I like to start broad, by giving kids examples of things that they can observe. Let's look out the window. The sky is blue and the sun is shining. Is it possible that there will be rain in the next few seconds? Possible but neeeeearly impossible. What about aliens landing in our driveway and knocking on the door to say hello? Likely impossible. And so on. Give lots of examples and then go Socratic to elicit examples from your kid.

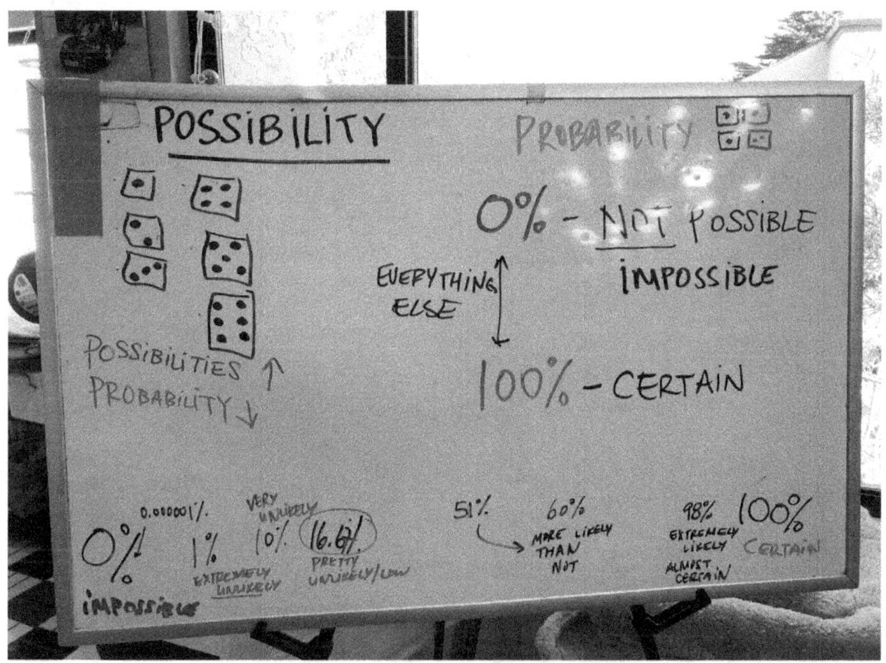

You can draw a scale on the board, and start to work in really basic percentages at the extremes. "When we say something is impossible that means there's a 0% chance of it happening. When we say something is not only possible, but certain, there's a 100% chance of it happening. Most things are somewhere in between."

Take out a single die, and ask, "Is it possible to roll a seven with this die?" No, it's impossible of course because there is no number seven on it. It only has numbers one through six. "What about rolling a zero?" Same. Impossible. Now take two dice. "Is it possible to roll a one with two dice? No, impossible, because the lowest combination you can roll is two, 'snake eyes'." By the way, kids love the expression 'snake eyes' and they will not forget it.

Probability With Dice

Since I believe gambling is such a compelling teaching tool for kids, I used all the gambling supplies at my disposal. We took two dice and actually drew out all the possibilities that could come up. Dov had fun with this and enjoyed drawing the dice. After we put them all on the board, we began to calculate the probabilities of any given number. It was much easier to visualize when you could count the different ways a seven could appear, for example. When you go through and find all the possibilities, you can turn them into the probability fraction of rolling any given number. Write those fractions out on the board, and diligently walk through the probabilities with your kid. Go back to the Pirate Ship example. The pirates tell you that you will live with any roll of the dice. *Except* you have to pick two numbers NOT to roll. Those two numbers would mean you walk the plank. Which numbers would you pick? Really guide them through this example to help them understand that they need to pick on the numbers with the lowest chance of appearing.

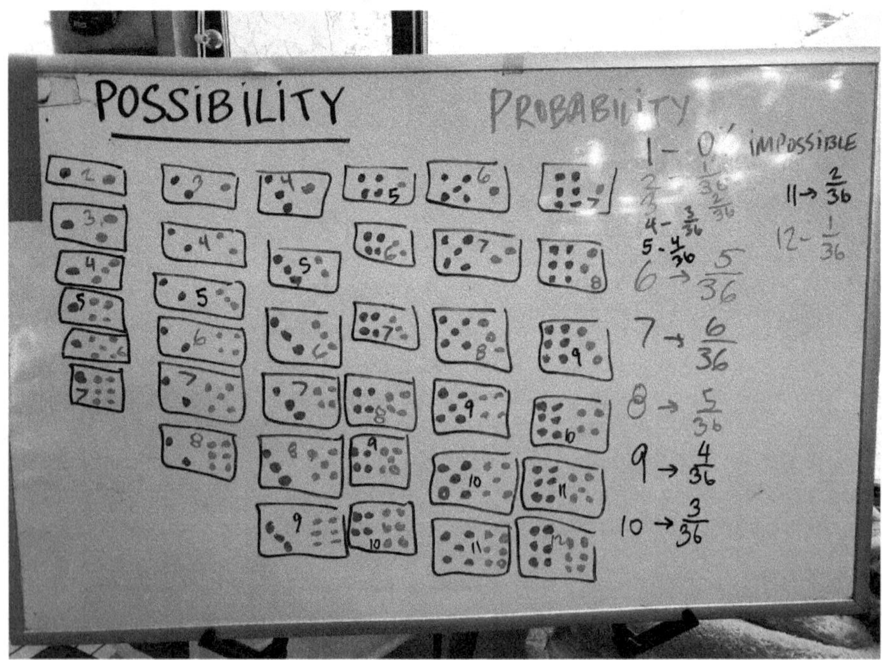

The Probability Board Game

I came up with this game on the fly as a way of really bringing it all together. Of course the prize is candy, so the kids are extra motivated.

This is a really flexible game, and you can tailor it to how well your kid is grasping the concept, as well as to the tools you have at your disposal.

Essentially, the game board has several train stops, and each kid can move forwards or backwards depending on the choices they make, and their subsequent luck. On their turn, they can choose to play one of four probability games. Here we used:

1. Heads or tails - if they flip heads on a coin, they advance. Tails, they stay put.

2. They pick a colored ping pong ball from a bag with three blue and one orange ball. Orange ball they advance two stops, blue ball they stay put.

3. They pull a card form the deck. Red - they advance one stop; Club - they stay put; Spade - they go back a spot; Q/K/A of Hearts - they advance two stops.

4. Roll two dice - anything but seven, they advance a stop. Seven - they go back one.

At the end of the line, there's a pack of organic gummy bears waiting for the winner.

There's no way to play this game perfectly on the spot. Even for an average adult, it's very difficult to calculate the probabilities of each option in your head. I made the choices up without calculating their odds first - the point was to give the kids lots of variety, and to get them familiar with how different games of chance can work. You can tweak these choice to whatever you think your kid will grasp. Start easy by doing a coin flip and the roll of a single die, or pulling one of three balls out of a bag, where one is a different color. Make the right choice really obvious. Remind them about the Pirates. As you keep playing, continue to increase the complexity of the options, and even ask your kid to design them. Give them ownership!

Advanced Lessons - Adding and Multiplying Probabilities

Once you feel your kid has a good foundation on probability, fractions, and the different tools of chance, you can push further. In order parlay probabilities, obviously your kid will have to have a good grasp of multiplication. This book is meant to be cherry picked, so if you haven't done multiplication yet, head over to the multiplication section and come back here when you're ready.

What is the probability that you will flip heads twice in a row? Three times? Four times? Etc. The coin is a perfect example because the denominator is small and it's fairly easy to multiply 2x2x2, etc. The cool thing about the interconnectedness of these lessons is that this could remind your kid of the doubling of rice on the chessboard (see Chapter 7, Double).

Now you play two different games of chance at the same time. You flip a coin, and you pick one of two colored balls, orange and blue, out of a hat. What is the probability you flip heads and pick orange? Explain that since the coin and balls are separate games, and don't affect each other, you can add the numerators and denominators in this case.

What is the probability of rolling a six and then rolling a six again on a die? Compare that to the probability of rolling a six on a single turn.

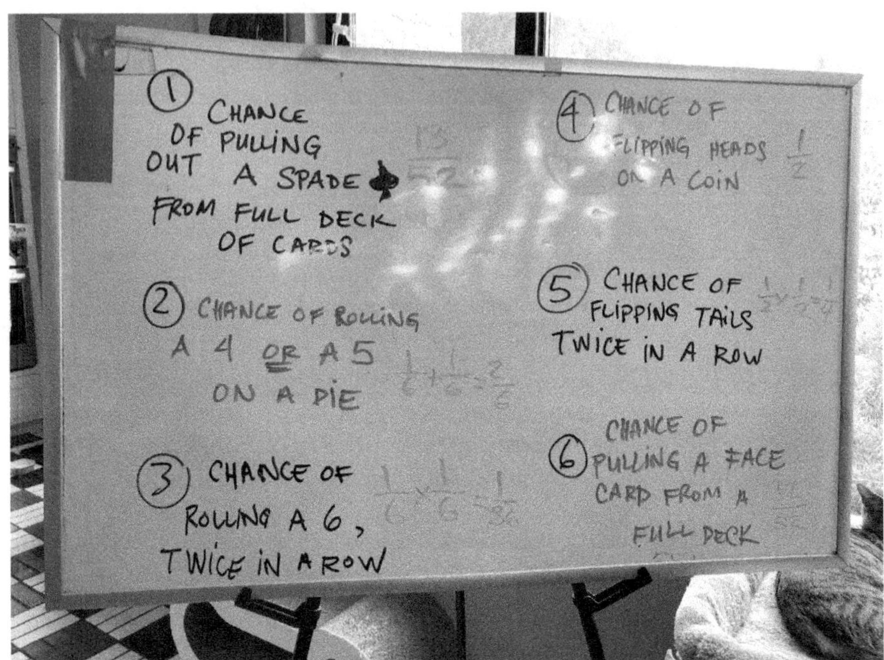

The beautiful thing about probability is that you can skip around and return to this topic again and again. You can opportunistically bring up probability and possibility when you're on a road trip. If you just left In-N-Out, what is the probability of another In-N-Out at the next exit? Is it high or low? If we just left San Francisco, is it possible that we will get to San Diego in the next five minutes? No! Impossible. And so on. As with anything in this book, once you've introduced these concepts, don't let them wither and be forgotten. Keep finding fresh opportunities to reintroduce and reinforce.

6. VOCABULARY

I remember studying vocabulary flash cards when I was preparing for the SAT. So when I started working with Dov on vocabulary, my first instinct was to resort to flash cards. It worked pretty well, but I could see that, if unrehearsed, his memory of about half the words would fade after just a few days.

I came up with three new approaches: (1) a salvo of similar-sounding, same-ending, or related words (2) opposite words (3) a deep dive on a single word.

My first successful experiment was to each the trio of words that have to do with opacity:

Transparent
Translucent
Opaque

These were really easy to demonstrate with tupperware containers from my kitchen drawer. I also used helpful mnemonics like: "When your parent expects you to be truthful - transparent."

Another successful experiment was the "Skittle Lesson". One of the kids brought a bag of Skittles candy to our pod. Initially I was pretty surly about that, since I'm not a fan of kids eating candy and junk food for lunch (more on that in the Nutrition chapter). But then I realized it was an opportunity. The word Skittle has the "LE" ending which makes this made-up word part of a unique subgroup of words.

I taped the bag of Skittle to the whiteboard, and called the kids' attention to the "LE" ending. Then wrote a bevy of "LE" words on the board next to it. I spent a couple of days going through defining and acting out these words, rapid-fire, with the kids. I didn't expect them all to stick, but it was clear that unifying them under the Skittles banner was an effective technique. Several days later, Dov had retained about 80% of the words.

I also combined the "same ending" and "opposite" approach to teach word pairs like Superior/Inferior; Interior/Exterior; Anterior/Posterior. Giving the example of two opposite words seems to really help reinforce the concept that's sandwiched in between. The kids especially enjoyed "posterior" for obvious reasons. Now, months later, I constantly remind fidgety kids that they must sit on their posterior. (Bonus: "posterior" is far preferable to "butt", because we all know what happens when that word is uttered in the presence of 5-year olds).

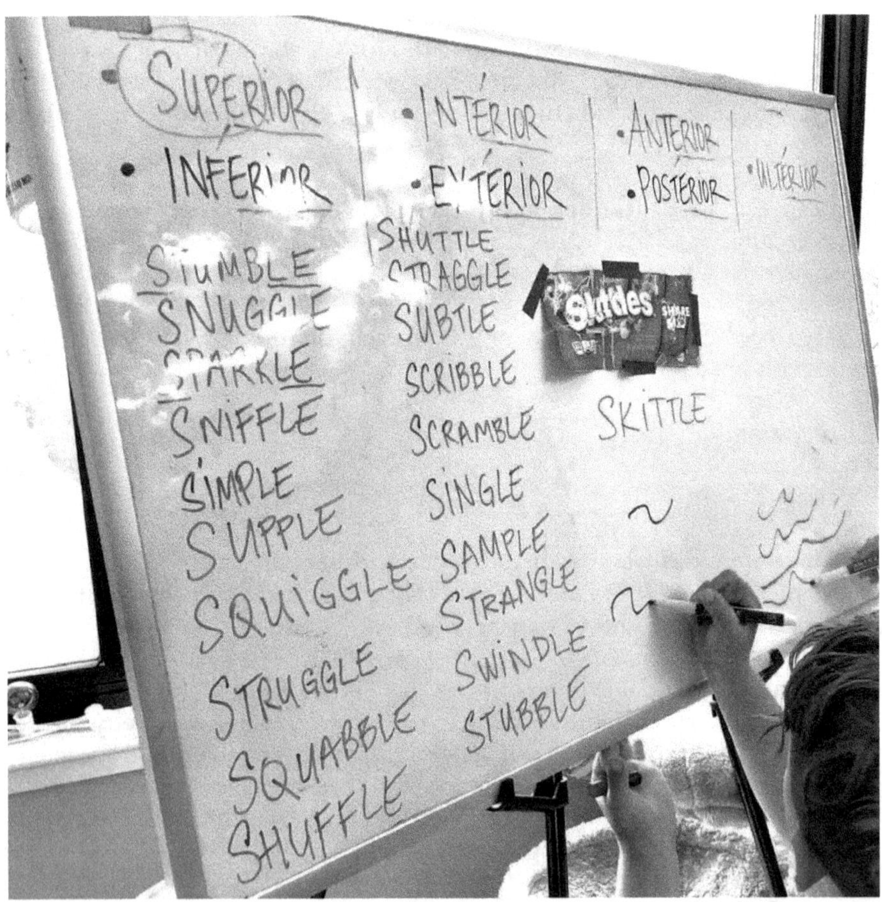

TION

Another very successful "same ending" lesson was about "TION". It's not easy for kids to understand why it should be pronounced "shin" while written as "teee-on". By exploring a whole group of words that end in "TION", it really helped to reinforce the concept. This particular lesson was so memorable for the kids, that months later, they'll often interject to point out a "TION" word whenever they see one.

Three Consonants

Another example of this type of word work was a lesson that combined "same beginning" instead, as well as words with multiple consonant sounds grouped together. We examined words that began or ended with three consonants grouped together, such as:

SCR - scream, screw, scratch
SPL - split, splinter, splurge
SPR - spring, spray, sprinkle
STR - strong, string, strum
SHR - shriek, shrug, shrivel

THR - three, throw, through
SCH - school, schedule, scholar
NTH - ninth, labyrinth, month

Grouping the words together allows for better memorization, and also helps reinforce the concept. Again, I found it helpful to get silly with making these three consonant sounds. I really exaggerated my lip movements and spoke slowly. I imitated a slow record, pronouncing the key part of each word as if in slow motion. The kids really enjoyed this, and it accomplished what I always try to do with the most difficult material: we made it into a sort of game.

An example of a deep dive would be the lesson I did on "Catastrophe". As you recall, I laid the groundwork for remembering this difficult word by asking kids to invent Dogastrophe, Pigastrophe, etc. Now, to follow up, I spent a solid hour asking them to recount what they would consider to be a catastrophe from their own lives. Moreover, I plotted the answers on a scale of 0 to 10, which is another favorite technique of mine (more below). I also gave some parameters, explaining what a "0" catastrophe would be (can't find a favorite sock), compared to a "10" (Titanic, 9/11). By using Socratic Method in this case, I really got the concept to sink in, and we made good use of repetition of the word. This was a particularly fun lesson because we got to riff a lot with the kids. They enjoyed making up their own catastrophes, and they intuitively understood the humor and sarcasm in a "socktastrophe", or a parent saying that the living room must be cleaned up b/c it's a catastrophe. It's truly amazing, and honestly, quite inspiring, that we could dedicate an entire hour to learning and examining a single word. I think the key to this was the sense of invention and play that pervaded the lesson.

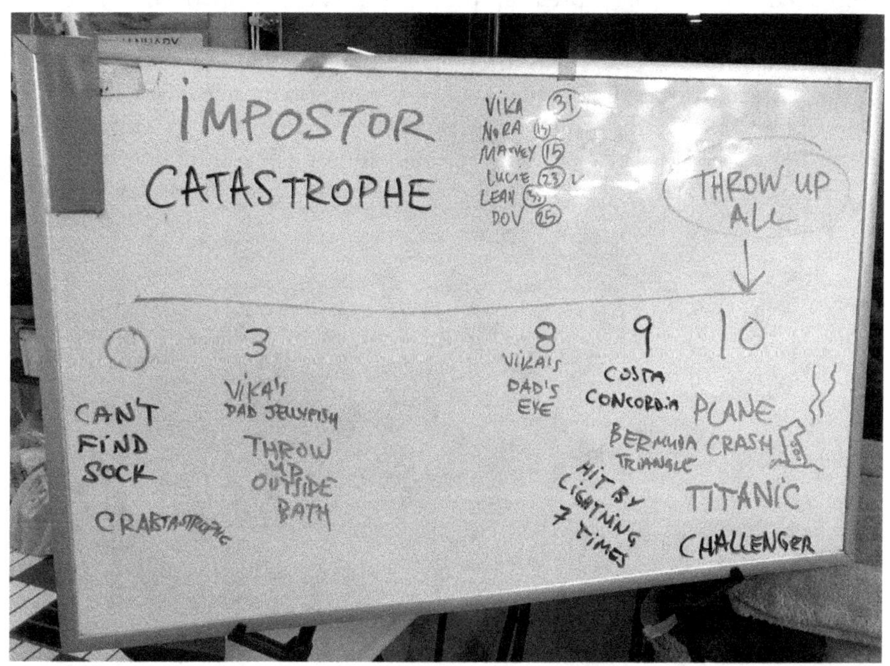

Common Prefixes - DIS and UN

You can make a basic introduction to prefixes. I began with asking the kids, "What does 'fix' mean?" Most of them were able to answer. Now I asked "So then what does prefix mean? Does it mean to fix something before it's broken? Like, Dov comes to me and says, Dad, I broke my NERF gun, and I say, it's OK, because I PREfixed it!" That got a laugh, and it was an important way to get the word "prefix" to get fixed in their heads. Of course then I explained that prefix actually means part of a word, that happens to also be the first part of the word, which changes the "base" or the second part.

Then I moved on to two really common prefixes, both of which do a similar action. Again, grouping similar concepts together. UN and DIS essentially mean "not" or "the reverse" of whatever thing they precede.

Then I gave examples of each word before we modify them with the prefixes. I used words that are mostly very familiar to the kids already, such as Safe, Cool, Comfortable, Fair.

Each time I brought up a new word, I asked them to brainstorm definitions, and then gave plenty of examples before finally adding the prefix. Then I gave lots more examples of the newly-formed word. I've already mentioned that I believe providing opposites / contrasts really helps to reinforce the concept. I also threw in a couple of words that don't quite fit the pattern, such as Uneasy (actually a suggestion by one of the kids) and Disembowel, neither of which really means the opposite of its unmodified form. I also gave lots of examples of each, and of course the kids really enjoyed seeing examples of Disembowel. Naturally, a lot of pirates were involved.

When I give examples, I try to be really animated and playful. Rather than just talking at the kids, I pick on them and use them in the examples. By repeating their names I get them to re-engage in the conversation, especially if I notice their attention wandering or tuning out. For example, for Trust/Distrust, I asked the kids to stand up, turn their back to me, close their eyes and fall backwards. Of course my hands were there to catch them, and this trust fall exercise was a great way to illustrate the concept of the word Trust, and its opposite Distrust.

Throughout the lesson, I really tried to weave the words together into sentences and stories, with lots of repetition to make sure it sinks in. Example: "I saw a big, mean kid walking around the playground and it made me feel uncomfortable and uneasy. I disliked and disapproved of his behavior towards the other kids, because he was acting like a bully. He was really disrespecting the other children, and doing a lot of unfair things. He pushed a kid down when he tried to get on the swings, while the other kids stared in disbelief." And so on. After you've inculcated this initial lesson, it's easy to build on top of this by adding more words in these categories. It also opens the door to working on other prefixes (re-, pre-, over-, under-).

Homonyms

I owe this lesson entirely to my next-door neighbor Debbie, who self-identifies as a strict grammarian (she even has a sweatshirt that proclaims "I am silently correcting your grammar.") She suggested that a lesson on homonyms might be useful for Dov, and indeed, it turned out to be one of the "stickiest" and most beloved concepts in his repertoire.

Homonyms, as we all know, are words that sound identical when pronounced aloud, but in fact are spelled differently. Prime examples of this are Two/Too/To, Your/You're, They're/Their/There, and Here/Hear. (Can you spot the opportunity to use the "opposite" method of teaching vocabulary that I describe above? Of course: Here/There.) After a couple days reviewing the concept, Dov was able to successfully do most of the sentence completions with the correct version of the homonym.

Homographs

A great segue from homonyms is homographs. A homograph is the inverse of a homonym. It's a word that while spelled the same, may have several different meanings. Just a couple of examples of homographs are Bark, Tank, Draw, Pass. Similar to the Skittles Lesson, I chose to throw a bevy of words at the kids and encouraged them to brainstorm different definitions. We really drilled down on the meanings of the words, discussed at length and even acted them out with the kids. Since Rake is also a homograph, as a reward after the lesson, I showed them a famous clip from the Simpsons where Sideshow Bob steps on multiple rakes.

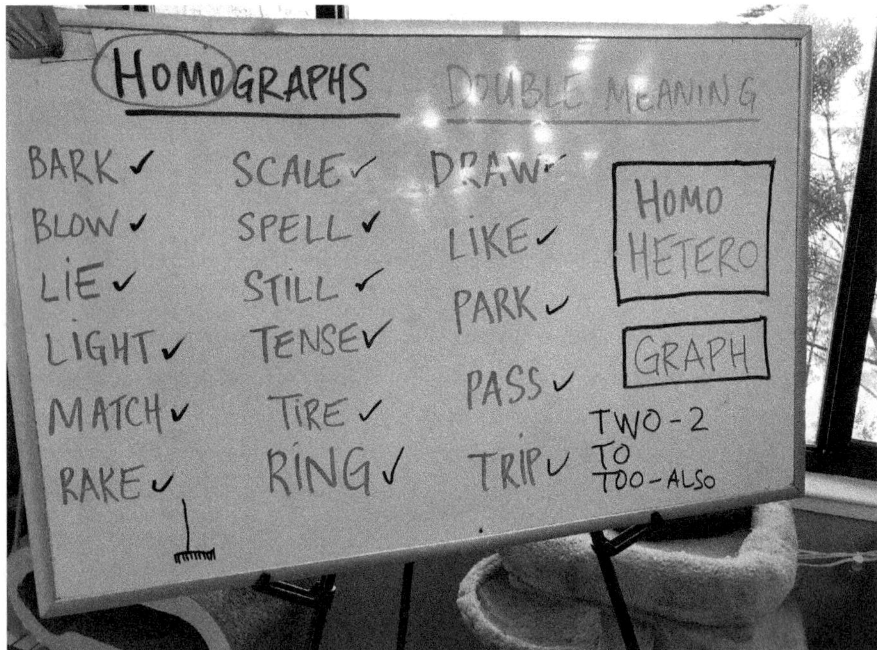

As with every lesson, there are several connection points and useful segues here. Homographs are words with a double meaning, and this lesson came on the heels of an entire week we did on the concept of "Double". It was also a great opportunity to teach the kids a bit of Latin, and explain what Homo-, Hetero- and Graph mean.

Building Vocabulary

From the very start of homeschool, I began keeping a vocabulary document (see Appendix A), where I keep adding all of the new words we learn. I don't expect kids to instantly memorize the new words I pitch their way, but keeping this list enables me to constantly go back and review. I try to pepper our conversations with the words we've learned, and I've developed a habit of winking at the kids every time one of the words comes up. It gives them a little cue, like, oh hey! There's that word! I think the kids really pride themselves on being able to remember and use new words correctly. I've already been talking about the various techniques I use to instill new vocab - using flash cards, batches of words, opposites. I also like to play hangman with the kids - it's a great opportunity to insert some new idiom or word that the kids then get to "uncover" and recognize.

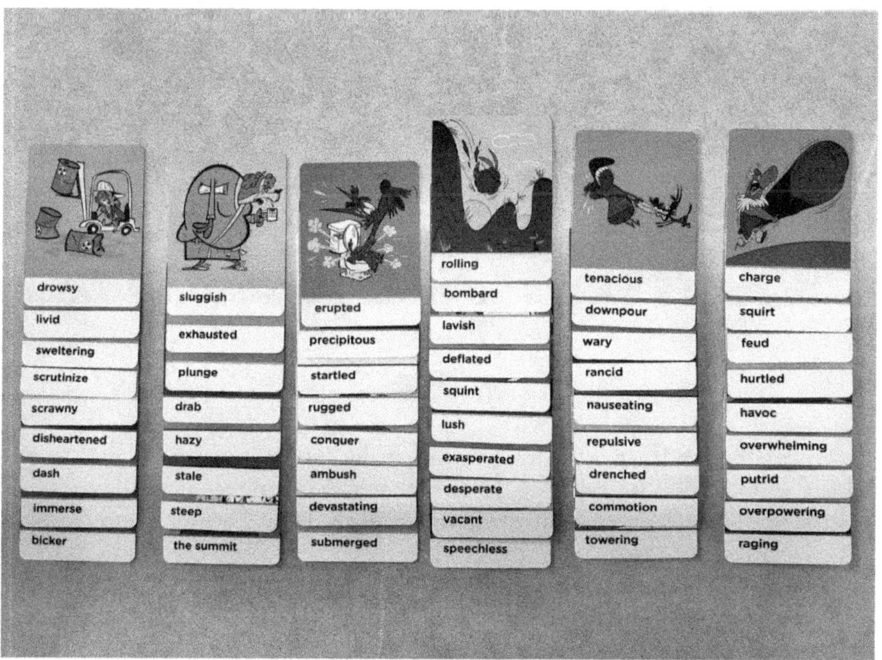

I opportunistically use themes to throw large pools of words at the kids. Since they are unified by a theme, it gives great context to each word, and helps the words stick. An example is when I used our Halloween celebration to discuss how different creatures move. It allowed me to review a whole list of interesting vocabulary words related to movement, without the kids getting bored. After all, each word related to a costume that they were already wearing. I even had them try to mimic each type of movement. For example, a zombie might Stagger and a mummy would Stumble. A superhero would Dash and a kitten would jump. And so on. Don't be shy about demonstrating the movements. Help the kids visualize it, and they won't forget it!

Word Scales

Another trick I use is creating "word scales": plotting words on a scale, which again gives a lot of context. For example, when we studied words that have to do with temperature, it was really helpful for kids to see how a scale might show words from the coldest to hottest. When we had our Halloween Week, we also studied "scary" adjectives, again plotting them on a scale from least to most scary.

SCARY ADJECTIVES
SYNONYMS
SPOOKY SCALE
FRIGHTENING
HORRIFYING
TERRIFYING
1
3
4
6
8
10
NOT SCARY
DONUT
SPOOKY
EERIE
CREEPY
BONE-CHILLING
BLOOD-CURDLING
NIGHTMARISH
REALLY SCARY
SPINE-TINGLING
HAIR-RAISING
ZOMBIE IN YOUR BED

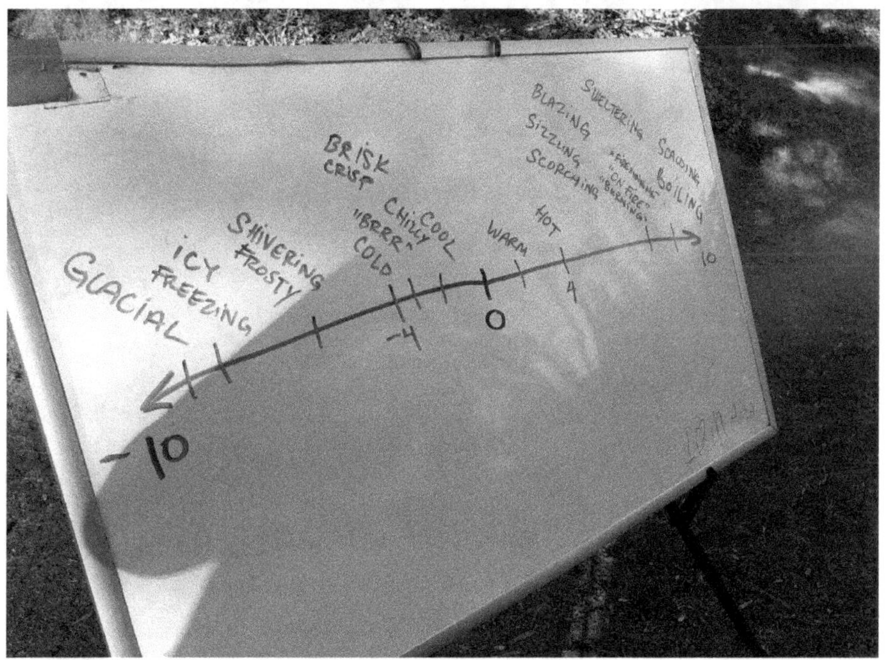
SWELTERING
BLAZING
SIZZLING
SCORCHING
SCALDING
BOILING
"ON FIRE"
"BURNING"
BRISK
CHILLY
COOL
"BRRR"
COLD
WARM
HOT
SHIVERING
FROSTY
ICY
FREEZING
GLACIAL
-10
-4
0
4
10

Onomatopoeia

One of the most fun lessons we ever had was learning about words that are also sounds. Boom, boing, clang, pow, splash, etc. are all examples of words called onomatopoeia, and they are incredibly fun for kids to learn. The kids really enjoyed going through my list of words, and they enjoyed making up their own even more. A great way to get creative. As you're coming up with the list, ask what type of objects would make these sounds. If your kid invents something totally ludicrous, don't let him just walk away from it. Try to get him to commit to (or invent) an object that would actually produce that sound. After you come up with a list of words, ask your kid to put them in context by using the word in a sentence. Even better if they can find a way to tell a short story that uses multiple words. Such as "The water balloon hit Timmy in the face, making a huge splat. Then came a splash as the water spilled all around him. Grrrrrr growled Timmy, reaching for his water gun. He aimed at me, and as I turned my head away - pew-pew-pew the water hit me in the ear!"

7. DOUBLE

I love exploring big "umbrella" concepts that can be applied to several areas of learning. Double is an obvious one, because there are lots of useful phrases and idioms with the word "double". It's also an important concept in mathematics, and a fairly basic one that you can get across to young kids.

We did an entire lesson on "Double" where we reviewed, and as always, acted out some of the more popular phrases. The kids' favorite was the concept of "double standard", since that's something all children experience daily when observing the behavior of adults (and usually, if they have them, the differential treatment received by their younger siblings). I taught the kids that typically the way to spot a double standard is if a situation makes you want to yell "HEY! That's NOT fair!" They really took this lesson to heart, and after "TION" it's probably the concept they reference most often. As usual, to reward the kids for making it through a challenging lesson, I showed them some YouTube compilations of cartoon characters and actors doing double-takes. (Tom and Jerry, Coyote and Road Runner are always reliable for this).

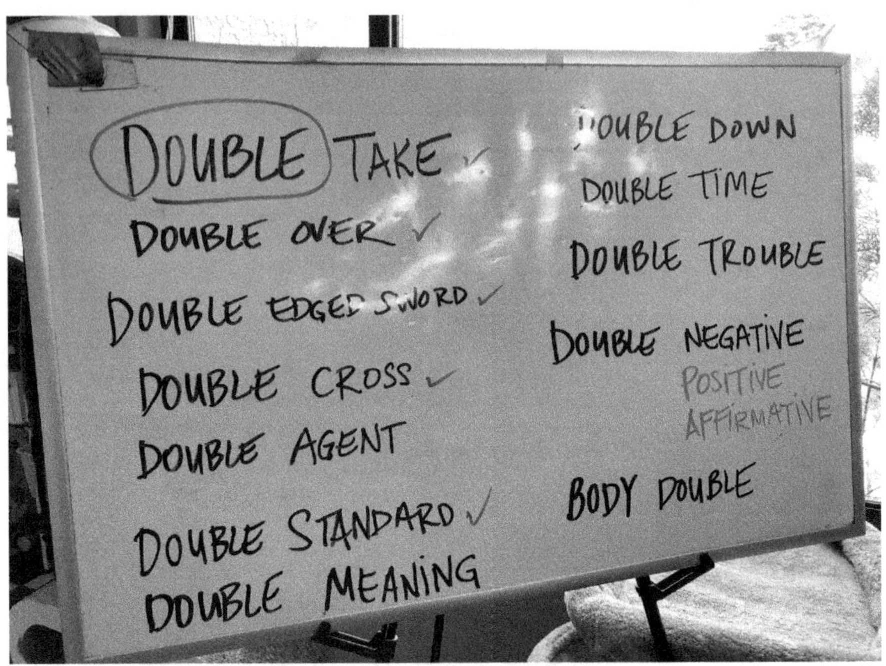

Demonstrating the idea of Double in mathematics was also some of the most fun we ever had. There is the old allegory of the inventor of chess, who when asked to name his desired reward by the king, said humbly, "I am a simple man. I don't need much but I could use some rice. If you could just put a single grain of rice on the first square of the chess board, and then double it on the next square and so on…". There is a fantastic video on YouTube by Let's Talk About X (search: rice chessboard) which visually illustrates this point, and after I showed it to the kids, they demanded to see it many more times. To take this lesson to the next level, you can start to introduce exponents. I explained simply that the little number on the top right tells us how many times we need to multiply the big number by itself.

Another useful way to reinforce the power of Double is to give an example of two kids: Timmy and Jimmy. Timmy is one inch tall, and with each passing day he adds one inch to his height. Jimmy is also one inch tall, but of course Jimmy doubles his height each day. What's really great here is that on day 2, Timmy and Jimmy are still both the same height. But of course, then their heights diverge very quickly. Finally, since kids are very highly motivated by candy, ask them to imagine that Timmy and Jimmy are their candy stash instead. Which "growth" of their candy stash would they prefer? Once again, we have an obvious segue to the more advanced concepts of Linear Growth and Geometric/Exponential growth. Even getting to a point where you can introduce these terms to 5 and 6 year old kids is a huge win. It was especially important for me to be able to communicate this concept in light of the COVID-19 pandemic. Demonstrating how a virus spreads exponentially was a great way to remind the kids why we are in such a serious predicament, and why it's important to wear your mask on the playground.

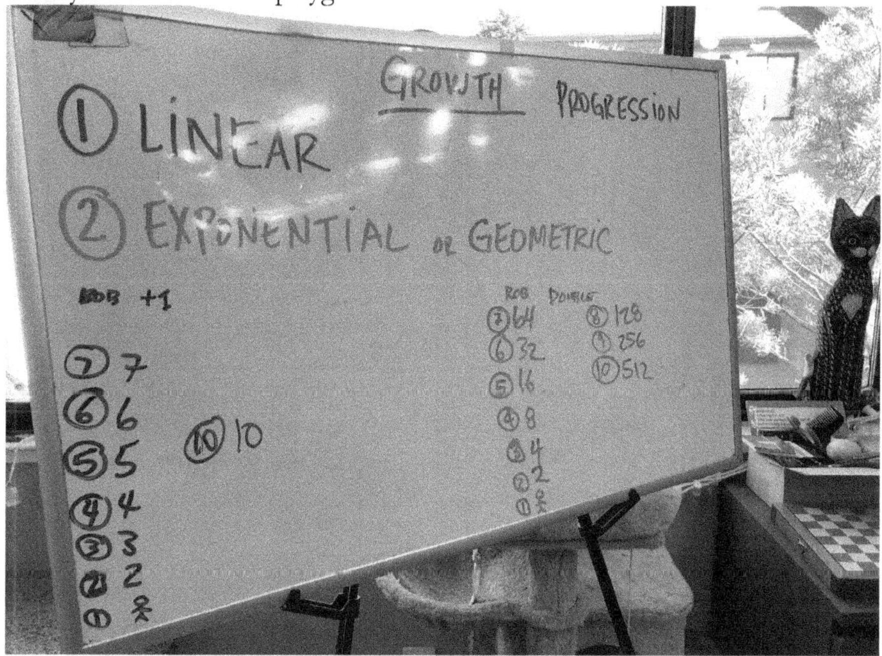

To further reinforce the word and concept of Double, I taught the kids the witches' spell from Macbeth. We learned the word "cauldron" and I had them don witch hats and cook up some "cauldrons" of their own.

Double, double toil and trouble;
Fire burn and caldron bubble.
Fillet of a fenny snake,
In the caldron boil and bake;
Eye of newt and toe of frog,
Wool of bat and tongue of dog,
Adder's fork and blind-worm's sting,
Lizard's leg and howlet's wing,
For a charm of powerful trouble,
Like a hell-broth boil and bubble.
Double, double toil and trouble;
Fire burn and caldron bubble.
Cool it with a baboon's blood,
Then the charm is firm and good.

8. IDIOMS

One of the most memorable lessons we did on The Green Schoolhouse - our online zoom class in the spring and summer of 2020 - was about idioms. The kids absolutely loved learning new phrases, and according to the parents, they immediately put them to use (sometimes incessantly).

There's not much to this lesson, other than to introduce some choice idioms and be really descriptive when you explain them. Prepare lots of situations where an idiom applies. Being a good actor obviously helps here, and it also helps to "put" the kids in the situations. This will help them relate and remember better. After you introduce idioms, find opportunities to sprinkle them into daily conversation with your kids. Whenever you plug one in, give your kid a little wink. Soon, they'll be telling you that you're barking up the wrong tree, and winking right back at you.

It's easy to google a list of idioms (I used http://www.idiomsite.com/), but below I'll put some of the most popular ones that kids absolutely loved.

Barking up the wrong tree
On the fence
Get off on the wrong foot
Got up on the wrong side of the bed
Heavy is the head that wears the crown
A drop in the bucket
A slap on the wrist
A taste of your own medicine
Back to square one
Cry over spilled milk
Water under the bridge

Don't count your chickens before they hatch
Curiosity killed the cat
Let the cat out of the bag
Put a sock in it
Till the cows come home
When pigs fly
Judge a book by its cover
Does a bear poop in the woods?!?*

*This is the kid-friendly, expletive-free version of the idiom.

9. IMPROV GAMES

I was really into improv back in my mid-twenties. The few years I spent learning and performing have really come back to pay huge dividends throughout my life. The concepts of "Yes and…", accepting offers, making your partner look good, and using play to break the ice have really been useful in my profession as a photographer, in my family relationships, as well as my new incarnation as a homeschool teacher. "Yes, and…" encourages us to accept another person's idea, and build on top of it. Accepting offers is the same idea. Imagine two improvisers come out on stage, and the first one says "Boy, what a nice sunny day!" If her partner says "Yes, beautiful! I couldn't think of a better day to be out on the lake with you, Susan." Now the second partner not only accepted the offer of a nice sunny day, but he built on top of it by setting the location and naming his partner Susan. The scene can now continue to develop. Now imagine the second partner responded "Sunny?!? It's raining! And it's not even day, it's almost nighttime." Now, the first partner is discouraged and frustrated. Their offer was rejected. The second partner made them look foolish for apparently getting the weather and the time of day wrong. So the scene either stalls out or turns negative. Even if the first partner tries to save it, she ends up getting defensive and saying something like "You know, you always disagree with me about the weather!".

You can see how relevant these simple concepts are to just about every aspect of life. They are certainly useful when educating young children. Teaching kids to be respectful of others' suggestions and ideas is no small task. Kids have strong little egos and they want to be first, they want things to be their way.

There are several improv games that are super useful for warming up and getting your homeschool day started. Some of them can also be played in the car or on vacation, so don't miss the opportunity!

I Am A Tree

This is a game that combines fun physicality with quick thinking. It requires three players. The first player comes up on stage, and strikes a pose that resembles an object, animal, or situation. For example, she gets on all fours, arches her back, and holds up one hand like a claw. She says "I am a cat." Now a second player comes in and strikes a different pose with a different idea. For example, he stands tall, making his hands into the "A" sign from the YMCA song and states: "I am a house." Now, the most challenging part of the game is on the third player. She must come in to the scene and transform herself into an object that connects the first two players' ideas together. For example, she comes in and stands over the "cat", pretending to hold a box with the cat inside. She says: "I am the new owner, bringing the cat home from the shelter." If you have more players, they can jump in as well. For example: "We are the kids, who are super excited about our new kitten!" This game is not going to reach a very sophisticated level with 5-8 year old kids, and at some point you'll start to see the most obvious ideas repeated, or it might just devolve into silliness. That's OK. Each time you play it, the quality of the kids' ideas will improve.

Three Things

This is a game of quick thinking. Also great to play in the car. All the players together say "THREE THINGS!". Then the first player challenges the second: "Name three vegetables." The second player must respond quickly with the first three ideas that come to mind. The response has to be quick, no "Uuuuuuhhhhh.....uhhhhhmmmm....". That type of hesitation will probably happen the first few times you play the game, but again, keep at it. After the second player answers, everyone once again says "THREE THINGS!" together. The person who answers then creates the challenge for the next person. And so on.

What Are You Doing?

Another game of quick thinking. Also, this game is great at teaching kids to do things deliberately and confidently. You'll see these words come up again in our lessons about chess. The first player comes up and mimes some gesture. The miming has to be clear and specific. If the movements are sloppy, they'll be impossible to understand. Let's say the player mimes brushing his teeth. Then one of the other players who is not on stage has to ask "What are you doing?" The player who was miming brushing his teeth must respond quickly, but cannot say "I am brushing my teeth." He has to say anything BUT the thing that he's actually doing. He says "I am shoveling snow." Now the player that asked comes up and relieves the original player. The asker now begins to mime the thing the original player said he was doing, which is shoveling snow. Another player now asks "What are you doing?" Anything but shoveling snow. "Jumping into a volcano!" And so on.

One Word At A Time Story

This is exactly what it sounds like. Several players tell a story one word at a time. Great training in listening to others, and expressing yourself in an articulate and coherent way. All kids know that stories begin with "Once upon a time…", so keep it simple and start like that. You don't need a large group for this activity. You can even play this game in the car with just mom, dad and kid. You may be surprised to learn that your kid thinks that "upona" is a word. So it would go something like this:

Mom: Once
Dad: Upon
Kid: A
Mom: Time
Dad: There
Kid: Was
Mom: A
Dad: Bird
Kid: Named
Mom: Abigail.

And now you're off! You've got a main character. The next level of this game is to explain story structure to your kids. There are a lot of terrific resources online for this, but the basic idea is that a story should have a beginning, middle and end. The story should have a main character. In the beginning ("Once upon a time") the character lives in some reality/ environment, until a conflict comes along and disrupts the character's life. In the middle, the character has to take on the conflict, which leads to new conflicts, relationships, and adventures along the way. The action of the story heightens during this time. Ultimately, in the end, the conflict is resolved and, as a result, the main character is fundamentally changed.

So in our example, we should explain where Abigail lived and what kind of life she had. Maybe she lived happily in a birdcage with an old grandmother. Then what comes along to challenge and shake up Abigail's life? Maybe the grandmother dies, or maybe the grandmother gets a new cat, or another bird. Take it from there.

Story, Story, Die

This is a great game to build on top of One Word at a Time Story. Here, you line up the kids in a row, and the leader of the game points to someone. Once they are selected, that player has to begin telling a story. As soon as the leader points to a new person, the first storyteller has to fall silent, and the new player has to immediately take over where the story ended. The gameplay goes on until a player fails to immediately take up the story, or if they hesitate or stumble. In that case they "Die!" and they have to sit down. The leader then picks a new player to continue the story and the game goes on. With young kids, these stories will probably be stunted and ridiculous, but that's not really the point of the game. This game trains kids to be unafraid of being put on the spot, and helps them practice public speaking and articulating ideas clearly.

Da Doo Ron Ron

This is a singing game, based on the famous, eponymous song by The Crystals. This game is all about rhyming and thinking quickly. It also teaches kids syllables, and the days of the week. Bonus! The song structure goes like this:

I met ____ (him/her) on a ________ (day of the week) and (his/her) name was ________.

[all sing "Da Doo Ron Ron Ron, Da Doo Ron Ron"]

The name of the person in the first line should be one syllable, and easy to rhyme with other words. For example, Jack (easy to rhyme with back, smack, crack, stack, whack, etc.) Abigail does not work here, because it's three syllables and difficult to rhyme, especially for young kids. So keep it simple (Bob - slob, knob, job, gob, mob; Ann - can, man, plan, ran, span, van). Also, all days of the week work because they are all two syllables - except for Saturday, which is three. So use this as an opportunity to go over syllables with your kids, and make sure they avoid Saturday. The song does not have to make sense all that much, although it's really cool when the song does end up telling a sort of story. The main idea though, is to nail the rhymes and maintain the structure.

So, back to the song. A sample song might go like this:

I met her on a Monday and her name was Ann.
[all sing "Da Doo Ron Ron Ron, Da Doo Ron Ron"]
She ate a strange dinner from a small metal can.
[all sing "Da Doo Ron Ron Ron, Da Doo Ron Ron"]
[all sing "Da Do Do Do Do, Yeah!]
First she ate, then she ran.
[all sing "Da Do Do Do Do, Yeah!]
Then she got hit by a van.
[all sing "Da Do Do Do Do, Yeah!]
That wasn't part of her plan!
[all sing "Da Doo Ron Ron Ron, Da Doo Ron Ron"]

Then the song is complete, and the next player goes. Ideally they will think quickly and pick a different one-syllable name, and a different two-syllable day of the week so that the rhymes will be different and the game will remain interesting. It's a good idea to plan this game around a lesson on rhymes. You can ask kids to brainstorm some one-syllable names, and then spend some time brainstorming rhymes for those names together. Write them on the whiteboard and then you can even reference them when the game is played. Rhyming is not easy for all kids, and so the key here is to not let them get frustrated. Help them along to get to a satisfying, completed song.

Twins Interview

This is a game that targets listening, teamwork, accepting others' ideas, and making your partner look good. It also works on spontaneous creativity, and if done right, can really lead to some priceless moments. Two people come up to the "stage" to play the role of twins. The catch is that when they speak, they have to do so in complete unison. In order to make this happen, both twins need to have ironclad eye contact, and they need to watch one another's mouths move in order to anticipate what the other person will say. Done right, this game leads to some really delightful moments. The rest of the kids pretend to be reporters, and they lob interview questions at the twins. This should start easy, with questions that have simple, one or two word answers. Do this first so the kids can warm up to the game. "Hey twins, what's your favorite fruit?" "Favorite food?"

And so on. Now, really encourage the twins to arrive at the answer together, speaking in unison. Usually, in the beginning, one or the other of the kids will "drive", meaning they will force the other twin to essentially go along with their idea. But the magic of the game is for both twins to sloooooow down their speech, watch their partner's mouth, and wait until a mutual word emerges. Inevitably you will get some predictable answers. Food? Pizza. Fruit? Apple. But once the kids start to get the hang of it, encourage more open-ended questions from the reporters, because this will elicit more surprising answers from the twins. Think behavioral interview questions. "Hey twins, tell us about a time when you helped someone." "Tell us about a time you felt sad." And so on. You'll find that some kids have natural chemistry with one another. Alternate and mix up twin pairs frequently, and encourage kids to be vocal reporters as well. Phrasing good questions in this game is just as important as answering them.

10. AUCTION.

The longer we did homeschool, the more I realized how much our lessons are interconnected. All it takes is one little spark, one little segue and off we go to a whole other idea or topic. "TION" got us talking about the word/concept of Auction. I then showed the kids some YouTube videos of professional auctioneers doing their verbal magic. The kids were enthralled. They demanded to watch again and again. They could not believe that a human being could talk so quickly. It then occurred to me that we should stage an auction with the kids.

Since kids are motivated by candy, I decided that this is what they'd be bidding on. But what would they bid with? The promise of sugar, and the excitement of the auction had to be earned. I dedicated an entire day to challenging the kids, both in the classroom and on the playground. They would earn their points for doing certain challenges or activities. For example, a point for each math problem solved, or a point for every 30 seconds they could hold a plank or hang on the monkey bars. At the tail end of the day, each kid would have X number of points, which they would then redeem for poker chips. Those poker chips could be used to bid on the candy at our auction.

This was a wildly successful concept. Not only did it motivate the kids to participate - and really strive - in every activity, but I also noticed how after a couple of auctions they began to develop strategy and perceive the value of an item. The kids started to notice that a fun-size Snickers bar is more valuable than a small chocolate coin. They began to conserve their resources and waited to make big bids on the things they really wanted. The most astute ones realized the value of not bidding early, and waiting until most kids had completely exhausted their resources and there was nobody left to bid against. Then, at the tail end of the auction they could buy even the best candies for a bargain. A "two-marshmallow" mindset, if you will. In contrast, in the very first auction, they were so excited that they pretty much bid on all items indiscriminately without much understanding of price, value or strategy. It was amazing to see this evolve organically. I gave no hints, and I was fascinated to see them figure it out on their own. Another benefit of the auction is that it sneakily reinforces the need to count correctly, since you always have to know how many chips you have to bid with, and you have to outbid your competitors.

11. GETTING KIDS TO LOVE WRITING.

I did my fair share of spreadsheets back in my corporate days. I remember really hating spreadsheets. What made it bearable, and even kind of fun for me, was the color coding. I was always doing conditional formatting, and meticulously color coding different cells and making my spreadsheets "pretty".

I think that writing can be a daunting task for kids, and here, as with math, small perceived failures can lead to big discouragement. Thinking back to my own colorful spreadsheets, I believe that writing should be creative, fun, and rewarding for kids. Therefore, I am a big proponent of writing with pretty, colorful pens. Glitter ink for bonus points. Also, kids should write about things they can relate to and enjoy! Kids love writing their own name. That's the thing they usually learn to write first. Whether doing an assignment, or just drawing a picture, you should always encourage your kids to write their name. They will do it gladly, and each time is a sneaky way to get them to practice their penmanship!

Quick Detour: I usually direct kids to orient their paper in landscape or portrait. After a few times, they have learned what these instructions mean and they orient the paper correctly. I also change up where they should write their names. Sometimes I say, "Put your name in the upper left-hand corner of the paper." Sometimes, I say "Put your name in the lower right-hand corner." And so on. The point of this is purely to get them comfortable with their lefts and rights, and to really start to know their way around a page.

Here's a sample writing assignment I did with Dov and a few of his classmates. Simple things that kids can get excited about!

One of the things I had the kids do was trade gel pens with each other after we completed each section. All kids love to talk about their favorite foods, colors, games, toys, drinks, best friends, etc. Birthdays, what they want to be when they grow up. Have them write about that!

Oftentimes kids will ask how to spell certain words, and I have no shame about writing them up on the white board for kids to copy. After all, the goal is to get them to practice writing their letters, and to feel proud of their work!

In this assignment, I especially liked Dov's experimentation with the comma and colon, as well as his proper use of the apostrophe. These had been fairly recent lessons, and clearly the concept of punctuation stuck with him.

No doubt 95% of the writing our kids will do in the future will be typed on a device. However, that's no excuse to abandon teaching them good penmanship. After they completed their writing assignments, I could see how proud the kids were of what they had written, and how excited they were to share it with their parents.

DOV YEVELEV

MY FAVORITE FOOD: IS
ICE CREAM

MY FAVORITE TOY
IS: HOT,WHEELS

MY BIRTHDAY IS: SEPTEMBER
26TH

WHEN I GROW UP,
I WANT TO BE A:
POLICE,OFFICER

I LIKE TO DRINK
KIDS' CHAMPAGNE

TODAY I FEEL
EXCITED

12. BASIC GEOMETRY.

Parallel vs. Perpendicular

This is a pretty simple concept to teach, but it has a high return on investment. Once your kid can comfortably grasp the meaning of these two words, they'll serve as a foundation for a lot of future math, such as geometry and graphing.

I recommend you start by giving very simple examples of what the two words mean. Something that your kid can easily visualize and relate to.

Parallel actually has the parallel lines embedded in the word, with the two ll's. That's a great place to start. Ask your kid to name a few things they can think of that are parallel. Help them along. Railroad tracks. The tabletop and the floor. The floor and the ceiling. The walls. Once you give a few examples, it will really open up their brainstorming and they should eagerly generate a few more on their own. It's really fun to see that "lightbulb" moment happen right before your eyes. The critical thing about parallel lines is that they must never cross. They can keep on going for hundreds, thousands, millions of miles, and yet they will never intersect. When I say big words like "intersect", I typically accompany that with a hand gesture, making an X with my hands. You can draw counterexamples of lines that will eventually cross.

Perpendicular is also fairly easy to explain. It's just a totally horizontal and totally vertical line that cross one another. When that happens, they form a letter T, or L (which can be oriented backwards, upside down, etc). Again I recommend drawing on the board to demonstrate, and also using your hands to show the "T". You can now move to brainstorming common examples of things that are perpendicular. The leg of the table and the floor. The wall and the floor. Your forearm and upper arm, when bent at a 90-degree angle. Two markers that form the letter T. Show a picture of an intersection, or draw one (and of course, make up funny street names, such as "Potato Avenue" and "Bacon Boulevard").

The most important thing with this lesson is to keep finding opportunities to reincorporate these concepts for days and weeks afterwards.

"Look at those two sticks on the ground! Are they parallel or perpendicular?"

"See how I am parking my car? It's called parallel parking. Why do you think that is?"

"Check out that swingset. See the pole that goes into the ground, and then the one that stretches across and holds the swings? What do you call that?"

Angles

A natural follow-up to perpendicular is to begin teaching the three types of angles: (1) Right (2) Acute (3) Obtuse. Here's where you really have to put marker to whiteboard and do a lof of drawing. Get your kid to do the same.

I liked using the mnemonic of my right arm, bent at a 90 degree angle to demonstrate a Right Angle. Keep reinforcing that any time two lines are perpendicular to each other they will form a right angle.

For Acute angle, it was helpful to do some word play. Since the acute angle is a "small" angle - smaller than 90 degrees - I called it "A Cute Angle". As in "awwwww, it's so CUTE!". Remember, if you make the example silly, and game-like, they'll do a much better job of remembering it. You can also incorporate the crocodile jaws. With an acute angle, the crocodile is small and "cute".

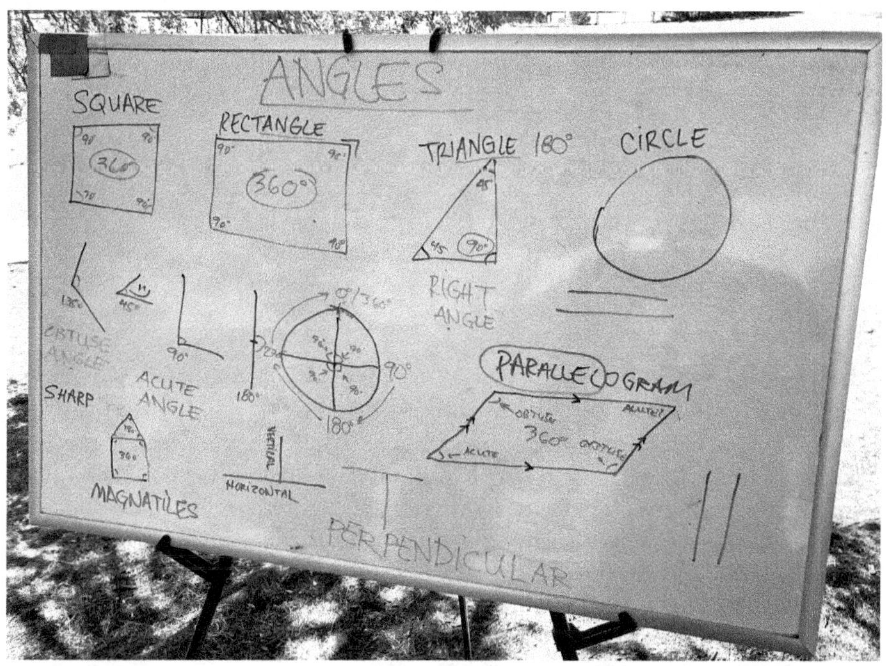

For Obtuse Angle, I found it helpful to give another definition of obtuse, which means "slow to understand" or stupid. Let's be honest, kids love put-downs, so as long as you do it in a joking manner it'll be a great and fairly benign mnemonic. We have a cat named Steve The Pirate, who is very fluffy and cuddly, but perhaps not the sharpest tool in the shed. So I made an example of Steve and said, yeah, you know how sometimes Steve can't find his cat food even though it's 2 inches from his face? He might be a little obtuse. I make an example of Steve in a joking, loving manner because I don't want to ever present a human example, which then opens the door for my kid saying something like that to another kid on the playground. We do, however, have a fictional kid we made up, named

Timmy, who constantly gets obvious things wrong (2 + 2 = 5). Timmy can be obtuse, and I suppose that's OK, as long as it comes with the caveat that we are just joking and we have to treat people the way we want to be treated.

Once you've dealt with the terminology, I recommend drawing some shapes and triangles and starting to label the angles. Hopefully your kid can count into the hundreds comfortably by now, in which case you can explain that inside a shape, the angles add up to a certain number (triangle - 180 degrees, square - 360, etc.). Make intentional mistakes and see if your kid catches them. My favorite intentional mistake was to draw a circle and then pretend to struggle to find the angles inside it. Expand to explaining things like a Right Triangle (has a 90 degree angle in it) as well as a parallelogram (called that because it has two parallel lines top/bottom, and two on the sides).

Once they start to understand these concepts, you can push further to have them do basic algebra using these shapes. For example: "If we know two angles inside a triangle, can we calculate the third?"

Shapes

Most kids know the basic shapes - circle, square, triangle, rectangle. I challenged Dov to draw more complex shapes - pentagon, hexagon, septagon, octagon, nonagon, decagon, trapezoid, acute and obtuse triangles, parallelogram. A good way to explain parallelogram by the way, is to have your kid imagine a rectangle that gets squished down and pushed forward, so the lines on the side become diagonal instead of vertical. A hexagon is two trapezoids glued together on their long sides. As your kid draws the more complex shapes with many angles, like an octagon, it's important that they pick up the pen from the paper as they complete each side. Otherwise their octagon will look much more like a circle.

The next level challenge is to creating shapes out of other shapes:

1. Can you make a trapezoid out of a rectangle and two triangles? (Or in reverse, can you make three shapes by dividing up a trapezoid?)

2. Can you make three triangles out of a trapezoid? (This involves drawing two diagonal lines.)

3. Which three shapes together create an octagon?

13. CHESS.

As I write this, The Queen's Gambit mania is sweeping the nation, and there seems to be a huge resurgence in the game of chess (at least if the ads in my Facebook newsfeed are to be believed). But I've always loved and respected the game of chess, ever since my father taught me to play when I was around 5 or 6 years old. I don't remember exactly when it was, but I do recall vividly sitting on the couch with my father as he was teaching me to play. After I lost the game, he knocked over my king as he announced "Checkmate!" (or "Maht!" in Russian). I was very upset about this, and I asked my dad why the king had been felled. He replied, jokingly, something like "Your king is sick and he can't get up." So I ran to the refrigerator, grabbed some nasal drops, and brought them back to administer to the poor king.

I played in some chess clubs as a kid, and I played casually throughout my life, but never pursued it seriously. I never really studied openings or end game theory. But as they say, "I know enough to be dangerous", and I felt I had a golden opportunity to teach our homeschool kids the game.

There are many books that provide an intro to basic chess, such as *Beat Your Dad at Chess* and *Chess for Children.* So I am not going to turn this book into a chess manual, because there are many authors and chess experts who have written far more effectively about it.

What I do want to convey here, is my own approach, and my creative ideas about how to get chess to "stick" with the kids, and how to get them to get excited about, and maybe even fall in love with the game.

I began using *Chess for Children* to teach Dov, but I quickly learned that teaching chess requires much more than a set of step by step instructions. It's a game of immense power and possibility, but unless your child is Bobby Fischer or Beth Harmon, and has a one-in-a-billion innate and instant love for the game, teaching chess requires a certain amount of excitement-building. I began by explaining to the kids about what makes chess such a special game. I referenced our lesson about geometric progression, and the apocryphal story of the "inventor" of chess and asking for double the grains of rice on each subsequent square. But the reality is that chess was not invented by a single person, but rather, it was molded and refined by centuries of changes, the way a stone is smoothed by the ocean waves. It coalesced from a game played disparately around the world to an idea and common set of rules that's shared the world over today.

It was important for me to explain this "stone-in-the-ocean" analogy to the kids, because it provided a very strong visual reference. I also reached back into our lessons on probability, to bring up examples of games of chance: dice- and card-based games, where winning and losing either completely or at least partially depends on pure luck. I explained that chess was different from all of these luck-based games because it is a game of pure skill. There is no luck involved. The best-prepared and most ingenious player wins. (I also did a little digression into luck, giving examples of "lucky" and "unlucky", leaning on the lesson detailed earlier about the prefix "UN").

Chess Directions

Since I was working with very young kids - ages 5 and 6 - I felt it was first necessary to review and establish some foundational vocabulary. Not all kids know what "vertical", "horizontal" and "diagonal" mean. Not all kids understand "forward" and "backward", especially when it's applied to a chess board. And lastly - this probably won't surprise you - many kids can't always tell "left" from "right". This is especially true for their bodies, since they are still developing proprioception. Telling a kid to stand on his right leg and raise his left hand can be very confusing. So first, I worked on a series of drills where kids had to step forward and backward, raise and lower their right and left hands, etc. Kind of like a "Simon Says" game, and there was a penalty for doing it wrong, such as three air squats or two pushups. I like to start the homeschool day with some sort of warmup, and this is a great one.

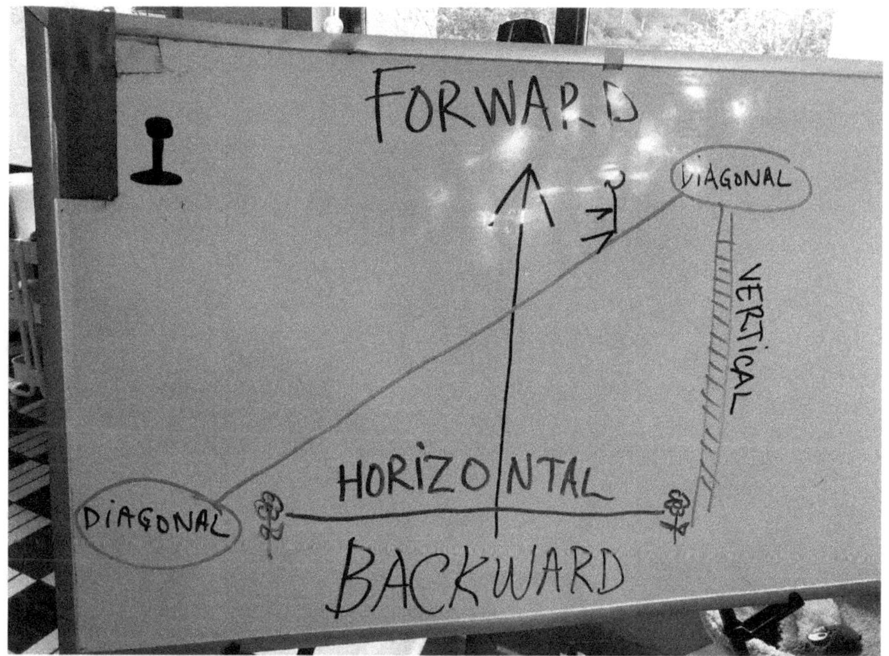

Next, we drew out a simple diagram to examine vertical, horizontal and diagonal. I like to give really obvious mnemonics to the kids, such as "the diagonal looks just like the slide on the playground" or "the vertical looks like the ladder going up to the slide" or "if there was a flower growing at the bottom of the slide, and another at the bottom of the ladder, then the line between those two flowers is horizontal". These foundational concepts need to be repeated and drilled until they start to feel like second nature to the kids.

Always be on the lookout for opportunities to reinforce the concepts you teach, especially when school is not in session. If you're walking down the street, and suddenly you see a leaning parking sign. What a gift! Encourage your kid to recall what you recently learned, and celebrate when they remember and get it right!

The Fundamentals of Chess

To teach the basics of the game, I created a really simple but elegant setup, with individual boards on separate tables, and a black and white barstool on the appropriate side. I also have a two-dimensional demo board which I always have hanging around so that kids constantly see the image of the chess board, even if we are doing something else. I use the demo board to teach remotely and also to do chess puzzles.

By creating an aesthetically-pleasing and inviting setup for the kids, I really encouraged them to dive right in and familiarize themselves with the game.

I made sure to get official boards that have numbers and letters, so that we could right away begin to prepare for writing chess notation. It's also a really sneaky way to get kids to learn and write lower-case letters. The 64 square board is excellent training in grid work. Getting the kids to identify squares on the board, such as "a3" and "h4" gets them practicing this ability to visualize the invisible lines meeting together on a certain square. Introducing the chess terminology of "rank" and "file" is also important here. Again, I believe that drilling is important here, and we practiced quite a lot of "find the square X". I explained the importance of the squares by comparing them to an address. "You know your address, right? Well, each square is a different address on the board. So by knowing how to identify the squares, we can tell where a piece lives, and where it moves to on each turn."

The foundations of chess notation offer a really sneaky opportunity to get kids to practice writing their uppercase and lowercase letters. I had them do this exercise, both to create a reference sheet for chess notation, and for them to practice their penmanship. As a fun bonus, I also had them draw the chess pieces on the same paper. I really inspired them to understand that magic of chess notation. "Imagine that two people sat in a cafe 200 years ago and played a game of chess, and wrote it down using this method. Now, we can recreate their game on our own board using their notes. It's like the chess notation has allowed their game to travel forward in time."

Using Battleship To Reinforce "The Grid"

Some kids have a hard time understanding how the chess grid works. This idea that each square has an address, made up of a number and a letter, can be elusive for some. A great way to reinforce this is to play the old school version of Battleship. Back in the USSR, we did not have the fancy plastic game with pins and plug-in pieces. If you wanted to play Battleship, you had to draw grids on paper. The nice thing about this was that you never lost pieces of a board game. It was ultra-portable and could be played anywhere. All you needed was a pen and paper. I encourage you to play this Soviet version of Battleship with your kids, because it not only teaches the grid, it also develops fine motor skills. Have them create, letter, and number their own grids. At first it will be frustrating, but you can use the opportunity to teach them to work with a ruler. This old-school version is a perfect complement to chess, since the Battleship grid is a 10x10, and the chessboard is 8x8. Battleship is a simple and fun game, even for really young kids. I started playing with Dov when he was 5 years old (at that time, I made the grids for him). If you can teach your kids to understand how Battleship works, then they will easily grasp the chessboard next.

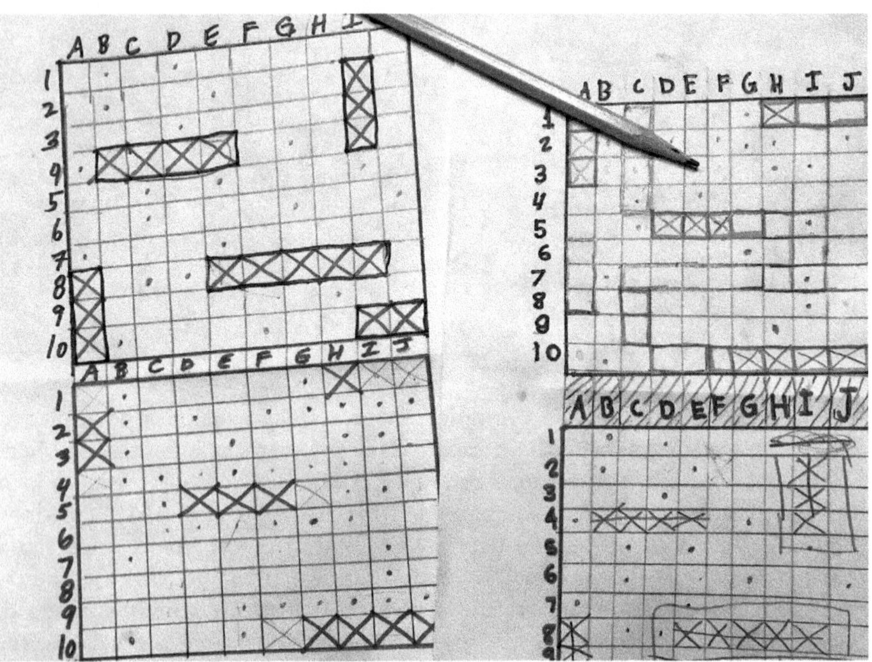

Moving The Pieces

A great place to begin is to go over how each piece moves, and why each piece is important. I tried to really anthropomorphize the pieces and have the kids do a lot of touching and feeling the pieces. I asked the kids to carefully pick up and examine each piece, to touch its edges and weigh it in their hand. We tried closing our eyes and really feeling the contours of each piece. I wanted them to fall in love with the pieces as if they were their best friends.

When first teaching kids about the pieces, I want to convey a couple of really basic and indelible ideas about each piece:

The Queen

> "The Queen is the most powerful piece!"
> "She can move any direction she wants, for as many squares as she wants."
> "She always begins the game positioned next to the king, but always standing on her own color."

The King

> "The king is the most important piece and must be protected."
> "He is old, and so he can only move one square at a time (but in any direction, like the queen)."

The Knight

> "The knight is the only piece that can jump over other pieces."
> "The knight moves and attacks in a letter L shape."
> "It is the only piece other than the queen that can attack 8 different squares at once."

The Bishop

> "The light square bishop and dark square bishops are like cats and dogs. A cat can never become a dog, and a dog can never become a cat. So the bishops must stay on their own color diagonals the whole game."

The Rook

> "The rook looks like a castle! They stand on the outside squares of the board as if they were castle turrets, protecting the army. The rook also has a special power, where it can do a sort of dance, and trade places with the king in order to better protect him."

The Pawn

> "The pawns are weak individually but strong together when they support each other. And they can magically transform - or get promoted - to another piece, even to a Queen, if they reach the other side of the board!"

I taught them how to set the board for the start of the game, and then as I felt them get comfortable, I played with the challenge of "Who can set up the pieces faster?" and pitted the kids against one another, as well as against myself. To make it extra fun for them, and to give myself a brutal handicap, I attempted to set up my pieces blindfolded. It did not go well but the kids loved it and found it very amusing.

"Deliberately and Confidently"

One of the fundamental rules of chess is that once you touch a piece, you must move it. This requires three things: (1) Assessing the board and really thinking a move over before committing to it, and (2) Not fidgeting with the pieces during the game (3) Once you have a piece in hand, moving it correctly and placing it deliberately and confidently.

Not surprisingly, all of the three requirements above are difficult for early learners of the game. Kids have a tendency - almost a compulsion - to fidget, and they tend to act impulsively. This is why chess training is actually a wonderful tool to teach kids patience and precision. I spent quite a bit of time reiterating this phrase, "deliberately and confidently". Pieces should not be dragged indiscriminately around the board, you should not clumsily knock over other pieces in the process. Think about your move. Commit to it. Move your piece deliberately and confidently.

Using Physicality

We all know that kids are fidgety little creatures and have a hard time sitting still. For this reason, I cannot require my kids to sit at the chess board for an hour absorbing theory. They need to occasionally move around and shake it out. When teaching how the pieces move, I will have the kids stand up and line up like pawns on the board. They will practice "pawn moves", either stepping forward one or two steps. By using their own bodies, they're able to better visualize how the pieces move. I'll ask them to move two steps forward and one step to the side like a knight. Or move several steps diagonally like a bishop or queen. Or capture like pawns and move one step diagonally. I try to deliberately trip them up, and say things like (as pawns) "move backwards two steps" (pawns don't move backwards). If they fall for it, they owe me 20 air squats. (The correct answer, I teach them, is to yell out "NO! We can't!!!") If they fall for it again, 10 burpees. Since kids have a hard time distinguishing left from right, especially when under pressure, I play this game with them too, asking them to raise their left or right arm, or stand on their left or right leg. Mistakes mean burpees. I also impose strict rules about dropping pieces on the ground. Kids know that the first time they drop a piece, they owe me 20 air squats. The second time - 20 burpees. And so on. All this air squat and burpee chaos kills two birds with one stone: It's a way for kids to move around and have fun while still learning about the game. After an hour-long chess lesson, I'll usually have a physical activity ready, like tag or a race, or we break out the boxing gloves and pads to give the kids a chance to blow off some steam.

Replaying Famous Games

Once the kids got comfortable with chess notation, I began replaying famous games with them. I used a two-dimensional board to demonstrate. First, I would introduce each game and explain about the players. For example, the first game we ever replayed was a match between Judit Polgar and Gary Kasparov. This was a great game to review because Judit Polgar reached an amazing pinnacle of chess - she became the top-rated female player in the world. She won this 2002 match against one of the best men in the world, Gary Kasparov, who himself had become world champion at the age of 22. Judit Polgar was a chess prodigy, but not in the way of the fictional Beth Harmon from Queen's Gambit, who seemed to just magically grasp the and excel at the game. Polgar's parents decided early on that they would train their daughters to become chess champions. Chess is a game where you can achieve a very high level through rigorous practice and memorization. Talent is just the cherry on top and that's what separates the greatest from the great. So this game between Polgar and Kasparov was pretty epic, because Polgar actually beat him. It's an interesting game, and Polgar's story also serves as a wonderful inspiration to girls.

To replay the game, I wrote down one move at a time, and had the kids do the same in their chess notebooks. This is an important exercise in staying organized on the page, concentration, and good penmanship. Writing chess notation forces the practice of both uppercase letters (N,B,K,Q,R), lowercase letters (a,b,c,d,e,f,g,h), and numbers (1,2,3,4,5,6,7,8). After each move I would pause and analyze the board with the kids. As the game developed and got more complex, I asked them to see if they could predict the next move, or provide the reason why Polgar or Kasparov may have moved a certain way. The kids found it very engaging.

We kept replaying games, including Adolf Andersen and Lionel Kieseritzky's "Immortal Game" from 1851, and the "Immortal Pawn Game" between Emil Josef Diemer and Thomas Heiling where the first 17 moves by white were all pawn moves! These are fascinating games because they break the mold of the chess rules I taught the kids.

Blunder vs. Sacrifice

What happens when you suddenly see your opponent seemingly give away a piece, by putting it under obvious attack? Should you act impulsively on this apparent gift and take the offering? I taught the kids that when they see this kind of situation on the board, they should first pause, stroke their chin and say "Hmmmmm." Because the "gift" may of course be a trojan horse. Perhaps your opponent really did make a ridiculously stupid mistake and gave away her queen. Or perhaps she's trying to distract you, or to deflect your piece so that she can follow through with a deadly plan? In this case, it would not be a blunder at all, but a carefully calculated sacrifice. I really wanted the kids to remember these two words, so I resorted back to our adjacent wordplay: "It's not plunder, like what pirates do; it's not thunder, like what happens when there's a storm; it's not under, like the sandwich that fell under the table; it's not plunger, like what you use to unclog a toilet ("eeeeeeewwww"); it's not blender, like what you use to make smoothies; it's BLUNDER!"

For sacrifice, I always like to use the example of throwing our proverbial Timmy into a volcano. I used this example in a lesson when we talked about how primitive people came to understand the world around them. I had explained that thousands of years ago, the primitive humans did not understand what controlled the weather, and so they ascribed it to some all-powerful being. And if it did not rain and there was a prolonged drought, they might have resorted to something drastic like sacrificing young Timmy into a volcano in hopes of appeasing the god and bringing rain. The kids particularly enjoyed that lesson because I would pick each of them up and pretend to throw them into a volcano. ("Do it to meee! Do it to meeeeee!") Since then, they never forgot it, and I always bring Timmy back whenever the topic calls for it.

I definitely used select scenes from Queen's Gambit as inspiration, and I could see that the kids were quite inspired by the game scenes. They also took umbrage at the scene where the janitor Scheibel tells the young Beth, "Girls don't play chess." They were very satisfied to have the janitor proven wrong in the epic season finale.

Opening Principles

Chess is a game that is learned by repetition. After establishing the foundation, I began to teach the kids opening principles of the game, with an eye towards teaching established opening combinations such as the Ruy Lopez, King's Gambit, Queen's Gambit or Caro Kahn.

To build the foundation for openings, I constantly reviewed and repeated several best practices of good chess openings:

- Develop your light pieces.

- Control the center.

- Have a plan (and see if you can figure out your opponent's plan).

- Castle to protect your king and develop your rook out of the corner.

- Don't take your queen out early unless you have a plan!

I kept repeating these basic ideas and asking the kids to repeat them at every opportunity. I figured that if I could get the kids to open the game correctly, it would make for much more interesting and engaging chess games with their peers and parents, which in turn would reinforce their desire to keep playing.

I issued the challenge to Dov early on that he and I would have to play one game of chess a day, and right away we began recording our games with chess notation. I created a chess notebook for him, so that he would feel ownership of his games. I think it will be very special for him to go back years from now and look at his first games.

As of the writing of this book, I plan to really push the game with the kids for the rest of the year. Dov already knows how to set up a Scholar's Mate, and I will soon be teaching the kids openings and some basic strategy. By April or May of this year, I intend to hold a small, outdoor chess tournament for our neighborhood, where both boys and girls will definitely play chess.

N Knight
B Bishop
R Rook
Q Queen
K King
X Takes
+ Check
++ Checkmate
O-O King's side Castle
O-O-O Queen's side Castle
O-1 White Loses
1-O Black Loses

DOV
CHESS
• 100 sheets
STAPLES

DOV VS. SASHA JANUARY 15 20,21

1. e2-e4 e7-e5
2. NH3 Nf6
3. NA3 b6
4. NC4 Bb2
5. D3 C7-C5
6. NXe5 Qe7
7. NCA D7-D5
8. NA3 NC6
9. F3 RD8
10. g4 H5

SCHOLAR'S MATE
e2-e4
BC4
Qf3
Qxf7++
e7-e5
NC6
Nd4

JP
GK
42. Rxg7 Kc8
1-0
a b c d e f g h
8
7
6
5
4
3
2
1

14. THE CASTLE LESSON: RATIOS AND ALPHABETICAL ORDER

I like to find an interesting and relatable theme that allows me to combine different disciplines into a single lesson. For example, our "Castle Lesson". Since we had been learning a lot about chess, the medieval was top of mind for the kids. So I reminded them that a rook looks like a castle, and then opened up a discussion about castles. What they are, why they were built, who used them, and so on. Eventually I steered the conversation towards war, explaining that castles were used for defense. Moats and drawbridges protected the entrance. Archers would be perched on the parapets and defenders would use stones and hot tar to repel attackers. After painting this vivid scene, I had them draw their own castles to get their heads in the game. You can also show some YouTube clips of armies storming castles (Robin Hood, Game of Thrones, etc). I usually don't give out screen time for free. YouTube clips are a reward for paying attention.

Ratios

Now I introduced the concept of ratios. "If you are an army storming a castle, you can expect that it will be very difficult to attack a fortified position. The defenders have an advantage: you have to come to them, and get past their walls and prepared defenses. So the attackers can expect to lose A LOT of soldiers in the process. In fact, a rule that military strategists generally followed is that you must have three times as many attackers as defenders, or you can say 'a 3:1 advantage'. For every one defender of a castle, there must be three soldiers ready to attack."

Now I've introduced the concept of ratio, and it's no longer some abstract math concept, but a very simple and easy to understand idea, even for 5- and 6-year olds. The next level here is to start doing some basic math: "Let's say there are 2 people defending the castle, Timmy and Jimmy. How many attackers will you need?" Build this slowly, with small numbers, until you can see clearly that your kid gets it. If they're cruising through the lesson, challenge with larger numbers and different ratios.

Alphabetical Order

After a challenging math session with ratios, you can segue, and give your kid a fun break by asking them to brainstorm things you might find inside a castle. Write the ideas on the board. After you've got a dozen or so words, the challenge is to have your kid put them in alphabetical order. This gets really fun when you end up with words like "archer" and "arrow" because they share the same first and second letter. Try to have this happen, because it will be a richer lesson if they can understand that if two words share the same first letter, you've got to move to the second to figure out which comes first.

15. DEBATE: DRAGON VS. UNICORN

One of our most successful lessons was a mock debate about which is better: dragons or unicorns. It's a natural thing to talk about, because unicorns are ubiquitous these days. Every other girl has a unicorn t-shirt, unicorn lunchbox, unicorn, unicorn, unicorn… Boys, for the most part, are indifferent to unicorns. But they do love dragons. So in this debate, there's something for everyone, although I like to mix teams up and make some boys advocate for unicorns and girls argue for dragons. Initially I ask the simple question: "Which is better, a dragon or a unicorn?" Most likely you'll get an immediate response along male/female lines, without any thought or explanation behind it. "DRAGON!!!" "UNICORN!!!" But as the kids know, my favorite question is "Why?". Once they spit out the first answer, I will then begin to explain that we really have to consider the pros and cons of each (and this is a great way to teach the definition of pro and con).

Unicorns are cool and pretty to look at, and surely you would be the most popular kid on the playground if you brought one. But unicorns are probably very high maintenance. You have to constantly brush and bathe them so they sparkle and look beautiful. They're not very bright, so you have to be very careful to make sure they don't wander out into traffic.

Dragons would not only make you popular, but also feared. No bully would dare pick on you if you had a dragon around. However, what would you feed the dragon? They probably require a cow or two every day. Where would you keep the dragon? What happens if you accidentally make the dragon angry?

These are just some ideas to spitball with kids. After introducing the concept of debate, you can then propose new ideas to argue about. For example, which is better, triangle or square? Black or white? Get creative. This also turns out to be an excellent game to play in the car on long road trips, especially because it's fun for clever parents, too.

Venn Diagrams

A Venn diagram is a simple and useful concept. Two side-by-side circles that partially overlap. Use this for comparing and contrasting two objects, concepts, etc. The aspects unique to each are in the non-overlapping part of each circle. The shared aspects are in the middle, overlapping section. Dragon vs. Unicorn is an excellent opportunity to introduce the Venn diagram. For example, high maintenance is what they have in common. Aggressiveness and a deadly disposition is unique to the dragon. Rainbow farts are unique to the unicorn. A fun challenge is to create Venn diagrams for two completely random ideas. For example, we brainstormed Vampire and Snowman, and brilliantly, the kids all figured out that what they have in common is that neither tolerates sunlight!

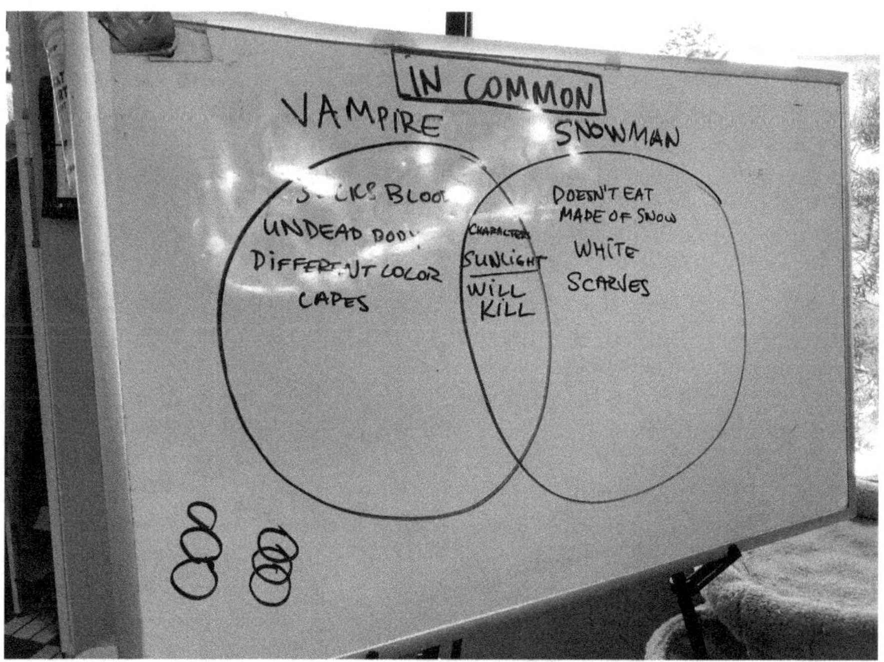

16. ELOCUTION AND TONGUE TWISTERS.

I observed very quickly that many kids have trouble pronouncing all the letters properly, even into 6 and 7 years of age. This doesn't seem to bother most parents, probably because the kids are still young and they figure it will resolve itself. My son actually worked with a speech therapist early on, not as an emergency, but more of a preventative measure. He was speaking two languages and we anticipated some issues and confusion around the different pronunciations. The few months with the therapist really helped him and now he has near-perfect pronunciation at 6 years old.

I began planning a spring show with the kids, and I used the preparation for the performance as an opportunity to work on their elocution.

I am not a speech therapist, but to me the obvious approach seemed to be to play with tongue twisters, and use that as our vehicle to motivating better speech. However, kids are not going to just do tongue twisters endlessly on their own. It's hard and kind of boring. So we needed to spice things up and, like pretty much everything else, turn it into a game.

I put 6 family-feud style cards on the board, each labeled with a different side of a 6-sided die. The kids would take turns rolling the die, and whichever side they landed on would reveal the tongue twister behind the card. I couldn't write the entire sentence on the board behind the card, so I denoted each with a simple word that clearly referenced the whole thing. The kids enjoyed this because it was more relatable, and also because for those who could read, the simple words gave them a sense of ownership and recognition. They loved the game, and it became especially fun when nobody could seem to roll a 4, so that card stayed unopened for several rounds. That made it exciting and suspenseful. Adding the element of probability was a huge bonus, because it gave the game life, and gave me an opportunity to also do a refresher on probability! It's all connected. Once the die was cast, and the tongue twister revealed, they would have to make several earnest attempts (with me repeating, correcting, prompting, cajoling). I carefully curated 6 easier ones first, and then once I felt like the kids were getting it (and also getting bored) I switched it up to 6 harder ones.

Below, I show the "keyword" that was hiding behind each card by making it all caps.

After a couple days of practice, I then offered the kids gummy bears as prizes to motivate them to try the tongue twisters on their own, and to do them successfully from start to finish.

First Round

1. I saw SUSIE sitting in a shoeshine shop

2. A big black BEAR sat on a big black rug

3. I saw a KITTEN eating chicken in the kitchen

4. SALLY sells seashells by the seashore

5. I scream, you scream, we all scream for ICE CREAM

6. Six sickly, sticky, simple SKELETONS

Second Round

1. If a DOG chews shoes, whose shoes does he choose?

2. FUZZY Wuzzy was a bear. Fuzzy Wuzzy had no hair. Fuzzy Wuzzy wasn't fuzzy, was he?

3. BETTY Botter bought some butter
But she said the butter's bitter
If I put it in my batter, it will make my batter bitter
But a bit of better butter will make my batter better
So 'twas better Betty Botter bought a bit of better butter

4. A SKUNK sat on a stump and thunk the stump stunk, but the stump thunk the skunk stunk

5. FRED fed Ted bread, and Ted fed Fred bread

6. We surely shall see the SUN shine soon

17. MEMORY GAMES.

Up In the Attic in a Big Black Box

When I first moved to the United States with my family, I was 8 years old and spoke no English. Someone arranged for me to have an English tutor come to my house, and she was the one who taught me this game. It has stayed with me ever since. The game is best played with several people, because it makes it more fun and challenging. But it can also be played with just two players, as I originally played it with my tutor.

The first person begins by saying "Up in the attic, in a big black box, I put a.... ________." Whatever the first person says, the next person has to repeat and then add their own idea.

When you first begin playing this game, the words should be simple, ideally just one-word nouns: "apple", "tree", "box", "car". As you and your kid(s) get more proficient in the game, you can start to get creative and even use this as an opportunity to teach vocabulary ("Up in the attic in a big black box, I put perseverance"). It's important to repeat "Up in the attic in a big black box" each time a player has their turn. It's a phrase that works on elocution, adds a nice rhythm to the game, and also injects more words that the brain has to remember, making the game more challenging.

So a sample game with three players might go like this:

Timmy: Up in the attic in a big black box, I put a TABLE.
Madison: Up in the attic, in a big black box, I put a TABLE, and a PEAR.
Brooklyn: Up in the attic, in a big black box, I put a TABLE, a PEAR, and an AIRPLANE.

And so on. If a player fails to remember, or fails to repeat the words in the correct order, they are out of the game. In the beginning, and especially in more intimate games, give your kids more than one "life". Let the game continue if they fail. Or coach them through it and give hints. As they get better, and more competitive, make the rules for failure more strict.

Matching Game

This comes in many forms, and you can order these games online. Basically it's a set of cards that has matching pairs. One side has an identical backing, like playing cards. The other side has unique pictures or words, with two matching pairs. We have a PJ Masks version of this game. I've also seen art history variants, as well as sight words and simple pictures of objects. Shuffle the card and arrange upside down on a table. One each turn the kids try to flip two matching cards, so they have to really focus, and begin to remember the position of cards that have already been flipped. If they find two matching cards, they take the pair off the board and it now counts as one point for that player. Play continues until all cards are gone from the table. Dov loves this game, and after some practice he has gotten quite good at it. Kids in general are surprisingly good at this game, because their little minds are uncluttered by daily cares and concerns, and they have not yet suffered the short term memory loss that comes from constantly checking our phones.

Mafia

For this game, you will need at least 6 players. It's a fairly simple but beautiful game that uses playing cards to assign roles. You can look up detailed rules online, but the basic idea is that there are a couple of Mafia (Queen and King of Spades) and the rest of the players are Villagers (low hearts) and one of the players is a Detective (Ace of Spades). You'll have more Mafia if there are more players. The objective of the game for Mafia is to kill all the villagers, either by killing off one of them each "night", or by getting the villagers to turn on each other and mistakenly vote a villager out. The objective for the Villagers is to suss out the Mafia based on voting patterns or a bad poker face. The Detective can ask the game leader each night about whether one of the players is or is not mafia, so he is a critical player on the Villager side.

To begin, the leader passes out cards, and all players discreetly peek at their cards. For young kids, this game is first and foremost about testing their ability to follow basic instructions:

"Do NOT open your eyes unless told to do so."
"No CHEATING and no peeking!"
"Do NOT fidget with your card and accidentally show it the others."
"Don't make unnecessary noise. This game is all about silence, subtlety, subterfuge and stealth." (Yes! Vocabulary words! Don't miss an opportunity to introduce new ones!)
"REMEMBER your card, and respond to the game leader's prompts when asked to do so."
"You MUST vote, but vote only once."

You'll find initially that young kids have a hard time with these basic instructions, but be patient. Don't reprimand too harshly when they drop a card on the floor or fail to remember their role. This is the point. Just be strict and gently remind about the rules, and start over. You have to be patient initially in order for this game to work eventually.

Once everyone has seen and remembered their cards, leader asks all to close their eyes. Now only the Mafia are asked to open their eyes, find each other and identify themselves to the leader. QUIETLY! Without giggling, without making a noise. Now mafia close eyes, and Detective opens her eyes, identifying herself to the leader. Now she closes her eyes. Now the village awakens (all open their eyes), and the floor is open for accusations. The players can accuse each other of being Mafia, and after a couple of strong, confident accusations have been made, there is a vote. Majority vote will force the person who was voted out to reveal their card. Before that happens, each accused has an opportunity to defend himself. This is actually an amazing exercise for young kids in public speaking (and doing so under pressure and scrutiny!). Once the defenses for the accused have been given, the village votes. Perhaps a Mafia is discovered, or perhaps an innocent villager is killed. In the first round, there's very little information to go on (although the kids will generally base their accusations on simple reasons, like "I saw her smiling really weird, so she must be Mafia!" "I heard him moving around when you asked Mafia to open their eyes!").

The next round, the Detective has an opportunity to ask the leader about one player's role. The leader silently acknowledges yes or no on whether that person is Mafia. The Mafia open their eyes and silently decide on their first victim. Eyes closed. Now the village wakes up. Here, as the leader, you have an important role to play in telling a compelling and funny story about the person that was killed by the Mafia, and how she was killed. "Last night was a dark and stormy night in the village. Late at night, and against her mother's wishes, Brooklyn rode her bicycle to the store because she really wanted to buy some cookies. Unfortunately for her, the mafia was waiting…" And so on. Mafia definitely wants to kill the Detective as soon as possible. Villagers have to pay attention to how people vote. Mafia has to vote carefully. Some of the nuances of this game are too complex for young kids, at least initially, but they pick it all up surprisingly quickly.

Repeat the process until either all Mafia are found out, or until mathematically the Villagers can no longer win (e.g. two Mafia and two Villagers are left, so the Mafia will kill a Villager on the next turn and the game is over). Look up the rules online for the proper ratios of Villages to Mafia, as well as other variants of the game that have more roles available. But for kids, it makes sense to keep it simple and easy to understand. The politics of the game are complex enough.

18. PAINTING WITH LIGHT.

I would be remiss if I didn't lean on my photography background for a lesson. Back in September of 2020, San Francisco had one of its strangest days. Smoke from wildfires filled the skies and created an apocalyptic, orange darkness. At 10:00AM, it appeared to be nighttime. I grabbed my camera and dashed to the top of Potrero Hill to get photos of the San Francisco skyline. But on my way home, I started thinking about what I would do with homeschool all day. The air quality was not good, and the darkness made me uneasy about safety, so the playground was not an option. If we were to be cooped up indoors all day, what would we do?

I decided to embrace the darkness and turn it into a fun photography lesson. I cracked open our Burning Man storage box and pulled out a box of glow sticks. With all of the lights off, the kids each received a glow stick on a lanyard. First I played some meditative music to calm the kids and enter a more spiritual and creative mood. Then, I set up a tripod and prepared my Canon camera for long exposure mode.

After a quick demo, I would have each kid try painting their name in the air with a little LED flashlight. I played around with 20-30 second exposures to give them lots of time. With a little practice, we actually had pretty good success! After the names, we moved on to painting objects: cars, flowers, animals. Some of these experiments were a total mess, but some actually worked! You don't have to wait for an apocalypse to try this out. You just need nighttime (or a dark room) a basic DSLR camera for long exposures, and a tripod to keep it stable. You can paint with really bright glow sticks, or an LED flashlight, or even simpler, the flashlight on the back of your phone! Regular glow sticks won't give you enough ambient light to make crisp paintings. You can see in the photographs how bright the LED flashlight is relative to the dim glow sticks in the background. If you want to achieve different colors with a flashlight or your phone flashlight, then you can put a little piece of colored gel plastic in front of the light source. Using a wider-angle lens helps, because it gives you more "canvas" area in which to paint. A portrait lens will force you to be very precise about where you stand in relation to the camera. Use something like f/8 at a minimum so that you have good depth of field in order to keep the scene in focus (again, widen your margin of error). Put the camera on a timer delay, and that will give you time to set up your position, as well as reduce any camera shake from pushing the shutter button - especially if you have the kids do it.

This lesson created some really cool photographic memories. I printed each kid's name and art and gave them the prints as a memento of that crazy day. I also think their minds were slightly blown by the whole process and the results! After all, they just waved a flashlight in the air for a few seconds, and here were real drawings. Very cool.

19. NATION AND LEADERSHIP.

These lessons took place around the 2020 presidential election. I wanted to give the kids an understanding of what was going on, with lots of context, and with no political bias.

Nation

"What is a nation?" I asked the kids. Let's take a step back. People live in a basic unit called a family. All the kids can relate to that. Families are different - some might have a mom and a dad, some might have two moms or two dads, some might have only one parent. A different number of siblings, or perhaps only one child. A family might be three to four people, let's say. Now imagine, thousands of years ago, when people lived in a primitive and dangerous world. Individual families realized that if they banded together with other families, they could be both more productive and better protected. They would be more effective hunters and gatherers if they worked in groups. In a larger group, they could also better defend themselves and their territory against other humans and wild animals. When enough families banded together in this way, they formed a Tribe. Perhaps a tribe might consist of 20 families, so say 60-80 people. (Good opportunity to use some multiplication skills here). That tribe would choose a leader. Eventually a nomadic tribe might settle down in a suitable area. The tribe would form an identity, perhaps using colors, songs, symbols, stories, traditions. Eventually several tribes would unite together to expand and protect their territory and resources against other tribes. This large group of united tribes could be called a nation. They've now come together under a common identity to protect their territory and resources, and they've chosen an overall leader, or perhaps a council of leaders to make important decisions on behalf of the collective group. The group may create specific symbols or rituals to identify their nation. A Flag is a simple national symbol. They might come up with a single song that their nation can sing proudly, together. That song could be called an Anthem. The nation would also need to create laws, or rules, that everyone must follow if they are to live together in peace. Some of those laws are very basic, such as "do not kill other people", or "do not steal other people's things".

Now, this is quite a simplistic explanation, but it offers a clear and concise way for five- to seven-year olds to understand the concept. As you can see, it also offers rich opportunities to introduce new vocabulary words, and even some math. (The vocabulary from this lesson can also be found in Appendix A, the vocabulary list).

We then transitioned to talking about the nation of the United States of America. I had hung up a giant American flag, and we turned our attention to the flag and discussed the meaning of the stars and stripes. We also listened to the national anthem, which most of the kids were hearing for the very first time.

Leadership

Now I asked the kids to pretend they are a nation, and they need to choose a leader. "Let's brainstorm the kind of qualities you would want your leader to have." To bring this discussion to a level that kids can easily relate to, I told them to imagine that the playground had a big bully, and that our group of kids needed to pick a leader to help protect our playground against the bully. The kids wanted their leader to be "strong", "fast", "someone that helps others", and "someone that eats healthy food". This can become a very interesting conversation, even at such a basic level. A leader is someone that keeps promises. Imagine your leader promises you a plan to stand up to the bully, but then the leader doesn't come up with anything. Or worse - doesn't even show up at all. Will you trust that person ever again? After a constructive brainstorm of leadership qualities, I made a segue to the looming election. Right now, I said, the nation of The United States of America is about to elect a new leader. People are deciding between two candidates. Who will lead our nation for the next four years? People are voting right now.

Fortunately, we have a firehouse with a polling station right next door, and so we all took a field trip there. We watched people cast their ballots, and the kids talked to the poll workers and asked questions. They were happy to share their newfound knowledge about the American flag, and about the kinds of qualities people look for in leaders. "Who did you vote for?", they asked the poll workers. "Can girls be president?" They walked away, proudly sporting *I Voted* stickers.

Building Their Own Nations

The capstone of this lesson was for the kids to create their own nations. I divided them up into two groups, and I asked them to design their own nations. They would have to create a name for their nation (we got "Nation of Fire" and "The Red Pentagons") a set of laws for their group ("no kicking", "no hitting", "treat other how you want to be treated"), as well as an anthem and a flag. They would also have to come up with ideas for how to punish people that broke the rules of the nation ("10 burpees", "no snacks"). Then each nation would have to vote for a leader, and that leader would be in charge of organizing a presentation of the flag, laws and anthem to the full group.

20. THE FIELD AND PLAYGROUND: GAMES, ACTIVITIES, IDEAS.

If you are fortunate enough to live next to a playground, you know what a magical world it is for kids. When the pandemic hit, we sought refuge on our local playground (despite San Francisco's misguided attempt to close them down). I found tremendous joy in watching kids play and explore and make new friendships and careen around like little ping pong balls. This is probably because watching kids play activates a deep nostalgia for the carefree adventures of our own childhood.

When I was a kid growing up in the USSR, I lived in a typical Soviet concrete apartment building. There were several buildings in our complex, and below them was what we - and all Russians growing up in a similar arrangement - called "The Yard". The Yard was where all play happened. You'd eat breakfast, go downstairs to play in the yard, and then eventually when it got dark, your parents called down from the window for you to come back home. I have fond memories of The Yard. Kids of all ages naturally intermingled there. The older ones would lead the pack, the younger ones would tag along. We obsessed over someone's new toy, we dug in the dirt, we played war with paper guns. We pretended. We imagined. We bickered. We made peace. We stomped through the fallen leaves and collected chestnuts.

In my opinion, a childhood is not complete without a "Yard" of some sort. Luckily, over the course of the quarantine, our local playground became our Yard. I am eternally grateful for the connections, adventures and friendships that have flourished there over the past year. All of us, and our children, were forced together by these unusual circumstances. All of us families made the pilgrimage to the playground almost daily. The parents kibbitzed from behind familiar masks, occasionally telling the kids how many minutes they had left of a particular activity, while wryly admiring our Groundhog Day-like experience.

For our homeschool, I immediately seized on the potential of the outdoors. During the warm San Francisco months of September and October, I set up camping chairs and a whiteboard, and held our classes outside. This had the added benefit of a small layer of safety (since the virus seemed to spread less effectively outdoors). But more importantly, it created a beautiful flow to the day. The kids would plunk down in their camping chairs, we would do a lesson, and then they'd be free to escape to the playground. After a nice mental and physical break, I would call to them, just like my parents used to call down to The Yard, and they'd come dashing back for another dose of education. Their brains seemed to work quicker in the fresh air, along with their metabolisms. It seemed that when we were outdoors all day, they were constantly eating.

I repurposed our old Burning Man cart to haul our chairs and supplies outside each day. The more activities I added, the more the cart overflowed with the various homeschool paraphernalia: Markers, mini-whiteboards, backpacks, lunchboxes and water bottles, balls, books, bands and even miniature barbells. Bungee cords held it all tenuously together. I would lug this cart out and back each day, sometimes fancying myself a 19th century immigrant peddler.

When I looked out at the playground and adjacent field, I saw only possibility. Ever since my son was very little, I always found fun and challenge in the everyday: "Bet you can't jump on that rock!" "Bet you can't walk across that fallen tree without losing your balance!" "Bet you can't sprint to that traffic cone and back in less than 30 seconds!" I always thought the simplest ideas were the best. Now I'll share with you what I felt were my most effective and engaging ideas for outdoor play. I had a group of about half a dozen kids, and I think this number also matters. You can do many of these things with just one or two kids, but a larger group makes for better motivation and also the possibility of making teams. You can always recruit kids from the playground if you need a bigger cohort. Usually that's not hard to do - kids are drawn to other kids who are having fun. Just build the game, and they will come! My games are simple and they don't require spending major money on equipment. A small investment in basic supplies will do. I will show you how easy it is to craft new games using the same equipment. Remember the auction? Sugar always wins. For all games, keep in mind that gummy bears are an incredible motivator.

Bandana Tag

Order two 12-packs of bandanas from Amazon, choosing two different colors. For example I picked orange and green. Let's use these colors as an example going forward. Divide kids into two teams, making sure that they're evenly matched in speed and aggressiveness. Tuck bandanas into the waistbands of their pants behind their backs, like tails. Now the game is simple: First team to pull out and capture all the other team's bandanas wins.

I make a point of trying to have teams matched equally in aggressiveness, because kids will react differently to this game. Some offense-minded kids will charge, while other kids will panic and retreat. This is a great opportunity to expose the more fearful kids to healthy challenge and competition. You can even encourage the more aggressive kids to "protect" their teammates.

Bandana Relay

Place six orange bandanas about four feet apart. Put six green bandanas in a pile, four feet behind the first orange bandana. Divide kids into two teams, making sure they're evenly matched in speed. Let kids decide the order in which they want to race. This usually involves some politics and conflict resolution, so be prepared for that. Once the teams are set, the relay works like this: First kid picks up a green bandana, races over to the first orange bandana, and replaces it, bringing the orange bandana back to the starting line. Now they grab another green and sprint to the next orange, replace again and bring back. Essentially the kid is doing line drills, until all of the orange bandanas have been replaced with green. When they come back with the last orange, now the next kid goes and repeats the process, except they replace the green back with orange. Keep repeating until each kid has gone. The team whose kids all finish first is the winner.

This is a great team-building activity. Kids will naturally be jumping up and down and cheering each other on. Inevitably kids will screw up and take off without a bandana in their hand, or they'll run to the wrong one, or they'll forget to replace one. That's all part of the fun, and you should encourage the rest of the teams to cheer on and help guide their teammates. Once I had a girl who got totally confused and just sort of froze in between bandanas, unsure of what to do next. In an amazing moment of leadership, one of the older girls on her team jumped out and started to coax her, running the drill with her, guiding her to each bandana and telling her what to do next. I hadn't made any rules prohibiting this, so I let it happen, and when the other team complained, I actually made a point of praising her leadership, quick thinking and out-of-the-box approach to teamwork.

Note: You don't have to use bandanas for this. We used colorful dodgeballs in the past. Bandanas are nice because they're compact and a cheap, quick order from Amazon, but you can use whatever you have at hand. Any two sets of objects: tennis balls and ping pong balls, markers and t-shirts, etc.

Bandana Retrieval

Place a dozen bandanas around the playground in hard to reach places. Up on monkey bars, on tree branches, on top of playground structures. You can either form teams, or have this be an individual challenge. Either way, use the stopwatch on your phone to time each kid or team to see how long it will take them to retrieve all of the bandanas. Note: safety first here. Don't put bandanas in places where kids might fall and hurt themselves. Know your kids and their abilities.

Bandana "Floor is Lava"

Spread out bandanas in squares across a field. Kids have to navigate to a specific spot by jumping and standing only on the bandanas. You can customize this game and use differently colored bandanas to add interest. For example, all are green except for two orange ones that are placed in such a way that makes them really hard to jump to. Hard, but not impossible. But if the kids can jump on the orange ones on their way across, that's 5 bonus points (or whatever). Another variation here is to make teams and arrange the bandanas in such a way that jumping across is impossible, unless one team member sacrifices themselves and lies down so that teammates can walk across their body. Younger kids will probably not figure this out unprompted, but you can try. Once you introduce the concept, it will be a lightbulb moment for them in terms of out-of-the-box thinking and also selflessness and teamwork!

Musical Bandanas

We are fortunate to have a carousel on our local playground. So we invented a version of musical chairs where the kids spin (slowly) on the carousel while I play tunes on the speaker. Bandanas are spread out on the ground at various points around the carousel. When the music stops they have to run to the bandanas. It works exactly like musical chairs - there are always one fewer bandanas than children, so each round someone gets knocked out. Safety first here: make sure the carousel spins slowly, and make sure there are clear paths from the carousel to the bandanas. You may want to bring a blindfold or just ensure the kids that you're closing your eyes when you stop the music, otherwise you'll hear a lot of "It's NOT FAIR!!!" A variation of this game involves putting bandanas of a different color. If you land on the green, for example, you are just safe. But if you land on the orange, you're still safe but you have to do 10 air squats, etc.

Tug of War

Timeless and fun. Get a nice sturdy rope that won't burn the kids' hands, and organize a tug of war. Kids against kids! One parent against all the kids! The variations are endless, and it's a great physical activity. The kids especially love going against a single parent, and they enjoy the process of falling down when someone wins. It's such a simple game, but it teaches teamwork, and if you do it right and tire the kids out, it expedites bedtime by 20 minutes.

Pendulum of Doom

This is a game that just somehow came to me when setting up Tug of War. I had my rope coiled up, with one piece of the rope wrapped around the coil, and stretched out about three feet. I suddenly realized that swinging the heavy coil back and forth by the three-foot piece created a pendulum, and I began to chase the kids around the playground saying "Beeeeewaaaaaare!! The Pendulum of Dooooooom is coming for youoooooooooo!" It was just a sudden moment of inspiration and creativity, but it led to close to an hour of fun for the kids. They loved running away from the pendulum, and eventually taunting it and trying to almost get hit. Since the rope is soft, even if the pendulum hits them, it won't hurt (which it should not do because you're swinging it gently back and forth). The key is to walk slowly after the kids, swinging the pendulum, rather than to create chaos by really chasing them around. They will be crazy and worked up, you should be slow, deliberate, and relentless, like The Terminator. Just walk at a slow pace, and repeat your lines while swinging your pendulum. They will love it.

Monkey Bar AMRAP Traverse

In CrossFit, there's the acronym AMRAP, which stands for "As Many Rounds As Possible". This is a simple game using that concept. How many times can you traverse the monkey bars without letting go, and without allowing your feet to touch anything for support?

Monkey Bar Dead Hang

Simple. How long can you hang on a monkey bar without letting go? For an extra challenge, make it a competition between the kids. Have two kids hang at the same time. Who will let go first? Usually the other kids on the playground will gather around and start rooting for one or the other competitor, which makes for a fun atmosphere! This exercise trains not only shoulder, arm and grip strength, but also grit strength. Is your kid able to persevere? Can your kid tolerate being uncomfortable? And finally, does your kid have the courage to drop down from the monkey bar when the hands can no longer hold?

Monkey Bar Banded Pull-ups

Few kids have the ability to do a strict bodyweight pull-up. But it's never too soon to begin training the movement. I use resistance bands to help. Loop a resistance band around a monkey bar, and have the kid carefully put her feet in the loop. Then, holding on to the bar, attempt a pullup with the assistance of the band. If the kid still cannot get chin over the bar, use a thicker band, or add another band, or give a gentle lift with your hands. The idea here is to give kids the feeling of success. Some stronger 5-7 year olds can do at least half a dozen assisted reps. Keep at it, and soon they will work up to a strict pull-up.

Monkey Bar Bandana Obstacle Course

Tie sets of two bandanas together and then tie them to various places on the monkey bars. Now the challenge is that kids have to navigate across the monkey bars without touching the hanging bandanas. If they touch, they have to jump down and start over. Again, know your kids, and adjust the level accordingly. You want to make it hard enough that they won't get it on the first try, but not so difficult that they'll get frustrated and give up. As with all games, this works best when there's a group of interested kids nearby, and the competition will motivate them to try harder and persevere.

You have to be a cheerleader as well. Throw out lots of encouragement and show tremendous excitement when a kid is making progress. You (and any other adjacent parents) should be jumping for joy if a kid succeeds in making it all the way across.

Jumping Over Stuff

Ever since Dov was a toddler, I would constantly challenge him to jump over or on top of things. Now, as a 6-year old, he has a 22 inch box jump. Part of it is surely that he's a big, strong kid. But the confidence to challenge himself to jump on higher and higher objects came from years of constant challenge and repetition. Challenge creates resilience, and effort builds confidence.

If you just look around, there are endless possibilities. Rocks, benches, curbs, steps, concrete blocks, boxes and so on and so forth. The best thing is, if you go to a gym, you can stack barbell plates on top of one another, and that allows you to gradually increase the level of difficulty. You should challenge your kid to jump on stuff that you know is a safe height, or that is safe to fail on. Here are some of our favorite jumping games.

Helicopter

Take a jump rope and swing it around in a circle, in a helicopter-style motion. (Think like a cowboy swinging a lasso). You should be down on your knees for this, which will allow the rope to be low enough for your kid. Every time the rope comes around to your kid, she needs to jump over it. This requires her to fall into a rhythm, and to stay light on her toes instead of making big heavy jumps. Big, stomping jumps will not give her enough time to recover as the rope comes around again. Make sure that the area is clear, because the last thing you want is for someone to walk into the rope's trajectory during this activity. Ouch. Challenge your kid to accumulate as many successful jumps as possible. If she trips, start over at zero. When playing with multiple kids, they all stand around in a circle around you, and each time all have to clear the rope as it comes around. When someone trips, they are out. If you want, you can give everyone a few warmup attempts, and then a couple of "lives" each to make the game last longer. This jumping game was so popular that each time I would bring a jump rope out, all the kids on the playground would flock to us wanting to play.

Advanced Helicopter - Carousel Version

If your playground has a carousel, the kind that kids can spin themselves on, you can attach a broomstick handle (we used extra bamboo poles from a home improvement project) to it for a more challenging version of the helicopter game. Now, as the carousel comes around each time, the kids must jump over the broomstick. The carousel height we have is about 18" off the ground, which is a pretty significant jump for the kids. Safety is critical in this game: do not spin the carousel faster than your kids can keep a rhythm. If your kid feels like he cannot clear the next jump as the stick is coming around, he should simply step back and out of the way of the radius of the stick. Focus is paramount. This game must be carefully managed. If the stick is coming around and kids are distracted, they can get hit in the shin or knee. For an even greater challenge, kids can do over / under. Jump over on the first revolution, then get flat on the ground on their belly so the stick passes over them on the second revolution. I've noticed kids really enjoy spinning the carousel on their own, setting their own speed appropriately. They figure it out pretty quickly. Still, this activity must always be supervised vigilantly. The playground is a chaotic place and kids can accidentally wander into the stick's turning radius.

Obstacle Course With Hurdles

I had a dozen leftover bamboo poles from a deck project, and I turned them into an obstacle course. By plugging 2, 16", U-shaped rebars into the field, and putting a rubber band on top of each one, I created "holders" for the bamboo poles, about a foot high. I spaced them approximately 2-3 feet apart. The idea is simple. It creates a series of hurdles that the kids have to jump over. Setting a timer is a great way to challenge the kids to compete against the clock and against each other. The key here is that each jump must be a two-foot takeoff and landing.

Variations on this obstacle course can include over/under, as well as a relay race where kids compete in teams. Another nice variation is to have the jump be sideways instead of forward facing. For added training, each time the kid jumps over sideways, you toss them a soft ball to catch and throw back to you.

Jump Over a Stick

It's amazing how little equipment you need to create a fun and challenging activity for kids. Take your broomstick or bamboo or closet rod, and place each end on objects of equal height (e.g. two park benches). Now you've got a bar that kids can jump over. You would be surprised at how engaging this simple setup is. One time, Dov persevered and accumulated 200-something jumps back and forth over the bar.

Obstacle Course for Time (no equipment)

Anything can be an obstacle course. You just have to use your imagination and the timer on your phone. "OK, run to that bench, touch it with your hand; run to the telephone pole, touch it with your left foot; spin around three times; do three pushups; sprint back to me and give me a high five. Ready, set, go!" In no time, your kid will be making her own obstacle courses, and she'll insist you participate, so bring your running shoes!

Design A Hopscotch

Bring lots of sidewalk chalk for this one. Idea is simple. Every kid knows hopscotch, so here they get to design their own. You have to lead by example in the beginning. The squares can be simple (jump with one foot, jump with two). They can also force the jumper to do different things: do a 180 degree jump, landing backwards. Draw some sharks, so the jumper has to do a broad jump over the shark-infested sidewalk waters, otherwise they have to go back to the start. Maybe there's a math square, where they have to do some arithmetic in their head before moving on. Or a push-up square or air squat or burpee square. And so on. If you haven't done something like this before with your kids, I recommend designing the first one together, so that you give them lots of ideas. Similar to the "Wake The Creature" Game, which you'll learn in a couple of pages, you have to set the tone. Once the kids get it, they will come up with their own out-of-the-box ideas. To give this game extra longevity, challenge them to create the longest possible hopscotch they can. Bring reinforcements of chalk, put on some music, and you have a solid hour-long activity.

Princess Dodgeball

Two teams. Can be as few as two people on a team, but the more the merrier. Additionally, each team has a "princess" (this does not have to be a girl). The princesses are placed in opposing corners of a field or a playground. Each princess gets a dodgeball (best if the dodgeballs are the same color, e.g. green). The green dodgeballs are for princess use ONLY! The objective of the game is to tag the opposing team's princess (with a hand, not with a ball to the face). The game is played like regular dodgeball - if you get hit, you're out. Also, the princess can defend him- or herself against would-be taggers, using the princess-only green ball. (If, in the chaos of the game, a player picks up a princess ball, they are out due to violation of the rules). The game begins with all the dodgeballs on the ground, and the two teams equidistant from the balls. (The green balls are not on the ground, they are held by each princess from the start of the game). On 3,2,1 GO! The teams race to collect dodgeballs and try to knock out the opposing players, and to tag the opposing princess while protecting their own princess. First team to tag the other team's princess wins.

Mummy

This is a game that was invented by one of my homeschool kids. (He was going through a mummy phase at the time). Basically it's a mummy-flavored game of tag. One person is the mummy, and they lie on the ground, or on a park bench, with eyes closed and arms folded across their chest. The other kids then have to invent a spell to wake the mummy. (It's more fun if they all say it in unison.) When the mummy wakes, the kids make a run for it, and the mummy begins chasing the kids around the playground. It's up to the mummy whether it staggers around like a mummy would, or if it's an extra fast mummy. Either way, once a kid gets tagged, they have to freeze and allow the mummy to stare into their eyes. The mummy then hypnotizes them, and turns the captured kid into one of the mummy's minions. Now the kid is on Team Mummy, helping to track down those pesky human children. However, if the helper kid captures someone, the helper cannot hypnotize. They must bring the prisoner back to the mummy and the mummy will administer the hypnosis.

Don't Wake The Creature

First, have the kids collect twigs, sticks, dry leaves, anything that will make a big crunch when you step on it. Now put them into a pile (the bigger the pile, the better the crunch). Now one person decides which scary creature they want to be. Variations have included dinosaur, zombie, vampire, "scary kitty", monster, mummy, and so on. Let the kids brainstorm their own ideas. The scary creature now lies down on the ground near the pile of twigs and leaves, and pretends to sleep. The other kids, now as a group, must quietly tiptoe past the creature. It's best if a parent introduces the first round of this game. As the kids are quietly tiptoeing past, you as the leader need to be whispering "Guys, quietly. Don't wake the vampire. Whatever you do, don't make a sound. We have to be extra, extra careful. Do NOT make ANY noise." As you say this of course, you have to deliberately make a big loud step directly into the pile, hopefully making a huge crunch. The creature wakes up and the kids run away, screaming with delight. Now, put the pile back together and have someone else be the creature (you should have no shortage of volunteers now). I recommend you once again lead, because you have an opportunity to make this game even more fun. Now, as you tiptoe past, one again, deadpan: "Shhhhhhh. Guys do not make ANY noise! We screwed up last time, so please be super, super quiet. Whatever you do --" and with that, literally jump and land as hard as you can on the crunchy pile with both feet, making the biggest and loudest crunch ever. Creature wakes up, kids are running away as they're squealing with laughter. Now, they get the idea. You may ask for a volunteer to help lead the group past the creature, but most likely you'll have a lot of eager volunteers ready to go.

Throwing - Paddle Catch

You know those velcro circle-shaped things you wear on your hand and catch a sticky tennis ball back and forth? It's called paddle catch. Those are amazing for learning hand-eye coordination, and for teaching throwing skills. Remember my indignation about the fact that many kids simply do not know how to throw a ball, or have no ability to catch one. This game really trains both of those skills. The kid puts the sticky velcro paddle on their non-dominant hand (to catch), and throws back with their dominant one. Since most young kids have a hard time distinguishing their left from their right, I usually ask "Which hand do you wipe your butt with?" It's funny, yet effective. They will look down at both hands and then make a quick decision. That's their dominant hand, so the paddle goes on the other one. Now toss the ball to them from some distance. Start close and eventually work your way farther back. Toss it gently and fairly high, to give them the opportunity to catch. Allow 10 tries, and with each one, say "0 for 1", "1 for 2", "1 for 3" and so on. Keep track. This will motivate them to get as close to "10 for 10" as possible. With more skilled kids, have them go really far away and toss the ball in a high arc in the air. This will really work on hand-eye coordination! You may find yourself having to calibrate your throwing skills as well. If you make a mistake and do a bad throw, immediately own the mistake and give your kid another chance! Otherwise you'll hear a lot of "THAT'S NOT FAIR!"

Bring Sally Up

Let's get the kids moving! This is one of two CrossFit musical workouts.

It requires a speaker so you can play music. Google "Bring Sally Up" and it will pull up the song Flowers by Moby. You can do this with push-ups, air squats, burpees, plank holds (straight arms to elbow plank and back). Every time the song says "Bring Sally Up", you come to the "up" position. Every time it says "Bring Sally Down" you go to the down position of whichever exercise you're doing. So if doing air squats, on "down" you are at the bottom of the squat, holding it. On "up" you stand up. It's fun if you mix this up with the kids, doing a different exercise each time you try. Encourage good technique, strong planks, no sagging hips or butts in the air. Good air squats, heels on the ground. Strong push-ups, elbows at 90 degrees at the bottom.

Roxanne

My favorite CrossFit musical workout of all time. Google "Roxanne by The Police". Every time the song says "Roxanne" you do a burpee. "Red Light" - air squat. Otherwise you're moving the entire time the song plays. Doesn't matter how. Dance, jumping jacks, jog in place. Just keep moving. This is essentially a high intensity interval training exercise, because there are two choruses where the action gets really intense. Roxanne...red light...Roxanne...red light...Burpee, air squat, burpee, air squat… You're going nonstop for like 40 seconds. Demonstrate good burpee and air squat technique to your kids, and encourage them to keep moving and finish the song! If done right, everyone should be splayed out on the ground, exhausted and gasping for breath at the end. Even though this is really hard, kids love it!

Nerf Gun Battle

At some point last year, Dov became obsessed with Nerf guns. For his 6th birthday, we asked all guests to get him a Nerf gun as a gift. I even did some serious research and put together a spreadsheet to make sure we covered all the bases. Big guns. Small guns. Bullets. Goggles. Vests. We inaugurated his Nerf arsenal by staging a massive battle on his birthday. Then, my wife Mila, in a stroke of genius, found a utility cart - the kind grandmas use for groceries and farmers markets. This cart really changed the game. It made it easy to store and transport all the guns, ammo and supplies out to the playground, unleashing us to host regular Nerf Battles for the neighborhood. Kids are drawn to the cart like moths to a flame. They revel in endlessly examining, organizing, loading, testing and trading the guns. Eventually they actually play, but they find equal if not greater delight in the process of preparation.

21. PERFORMANCE.

I looked at the big picture of what we had learned and accomplished over the past few months of homeschool. One thing was obviously missing: I had not challenged the kids to perform. I think the spring show, or school play, are incredibly valuable experiences for kids. They teach children to take ownership of a role. To take responsibility for preparing and rehearsing their lines. To play dress-up. It exposes kids to public speaking, and gives the opportunity for young kids to experience the rush of delivering a (hopefully) well-rehearsed role. If done right, it gives them a chance to experience the glow of pride in a job well done.

For many kids that are terrified of public speaking, this is an invaluable chance to venture out of their comfort zone. It requires a great deal of coaxing and sensitivity by the instructor. It may be intimidating, as the instructor, to take on the responsibility of pushing a kid outside their comfort zone. But, as the saying goes "The best time to plant a tree was yesterday. The second best time is today."

I sat down and wrote a script. About chess. The kids would be the chess pieces (well, one would play the chessboard itself, and another would be the chess clock). The show would be a fun, punny, yet informative romp. With humor that both parents and kids could appreciate. Even if the performance was a total failure, I figured that kids would learn a tremendous amount from the process of preparing for it. It would reinforce many of the chess concepts we were already learning, and it would give me a chance to expose the kids to lots of other ideas about shows and musicals.

In preparation, I put the kids through a sort of performance bootcamp.

We did musical warmups, breath exercises, and sang scales. I leaned heavily on improv games such as I Am A Tree and Da Doo Ron Ron. We learned about "I Wish" songs, where, in the beginning of a story, the main character expresses their deepest desires (For example, Simba's "I Just Can't Wait To Be King", Ariel's "Part of Their World", Tevye's "If I Were A Rich Man" or Hamilton's "My Shot"). We watched YouTube clips of these songs for inspiration. (The kids were, for some reason, particularly excited about Fiddler on The Roof).

I include the full script of the performance as an appendix to this book. I hope that future educators will find it useful.

APPENDIX A: VOCABULARY LIST.

"RGE"
Urge
Merge
Submerge
Emerge
Splurge
Surge
Purge

"TRANSPARENCY"
Transparent
Translucent
Opaque

"RIOR"
Superior
Inferior

Interior
Exterior

Anterior
Posterior

Ulterior

"VOLVE"
Revolve
Evolve

SCARY SYNONYMS
Spooky
Eerie
Creepy
Frightening
Spine-Tingling
Hair-Raising
Bone-Chilling
Blood-Curdling
Horrifying
Terrifying
Nightmarish

"S____LE"
Stumble
Snuggle
Sparkle
Sniffle
Simple
Supple
Squiggle
Struggle
Squabble
Shuffle
Shuttle
Straggle
Subtle
Scribble
Scramble
Single
Sample
Strangle
Swindle
Stubble

WHAT MAKES SOMETHING FUNNY

Absurd
Ridiculous
Unusual
Unexpected
New
Surprising
Silly
Exciting
Timing

MOVEMENT

Jump
Strut
Sprint
Crawl
Scoot
Prance
Prowl
Gallop
Trudge
Stumble
Hover
Bolt
Creep
Skulk
Dance
Zoom
Tiptoe
Stagger
Slither
Skip
Tumble
Amble
Traipse
Race
Drag
March
Accelerate
Decelerate

HALLOWEEN-INSPIRED
Defenestrate vs. Decapitate
Omen
Foreshadowing
Harvest
Bounty
Abundance
Lavish
Feast
Premonition vs. Apparition

3 CONSONANTS

SCR
Scream
Screw
Scribble
Scrape
Scrub

SPL
Splinter
Splat
Splash
Splurge
Splendid

SPR
Sprint
Spray
Sprout
Sprain
Sprinkles

STR
Strong
Strut
Stripe
String
Strum

TEMPERATURE COLD
Cool
Chilly
Brisk
Crisp
Frosty
Shivering
Icy
Freezing
Glacial

TEMPERATURE HOT
Warm
Scorching
Sizzling
Blazing
Sweltering
Burning
Boiling
Scalding

LEADERSHIP & NATION
Communicate
Command
Candidate
Elect
Reliable
Confident
Proud
Keeps Promises
Respect
Believe
Trust
United
Anthem
Identity
Territory
Resources
Tribe
Council
Laws
Nomadic

ONOMATOPOEIA
Boing
Sploosh
Splash
Pow
Clang
Ding-Dong
Whoosh
Zoom
Splat
Pew-Pew
Clink
Zap
Boink

NTH
Labyrinth
Month
Ninth, Tenth, Eleventh… Millionth… etc.

SHR
Shrivel
Shrink
Shriek
Shrewd
Shrug

THR
Thrill
Threat
Threshold
Throb
Thrust

SCH
School
Schedule
Schism
Scholar
Scheme

"TION" 1st 11 WORDS
Nation
Fiction
Imagination
Option
Potion
Emotion
Portion
Vacation
Lotion
Motion
Introduction

"TION" 2nd 11 WORDS
Solution
Situation
Commotion
Devotion
Auction
Action
Promotion
Demotion
Demolition
Objection
Exception
Negotiation

"TION" 3rd 11 WORDS
Tradition
Aspiration
Excavation
Repetition
Temptation
Suggestion
Assumption
Protection
Provocation
Indignation
Misconception

WORDS THAT MAKE YOU GO "HMMM"
Peculiar
Strange
Curious
Unusual
Wacky
Eccentric
Odd

"ABLE"
Able
Fable
Table
Stable
Cable
Enable
Unable
Doable
Usable
Viable

"THE WITCHES" ROALD DAHL
Encounter
Ordinary
Narrator
Adore
Fluent

LATIN
Homo-
Hetero-
Graph

DOUBLE
"Double double toil and trouble, fire burn and cauldron bubble..."
Double Take
Double Over
Double Cross
Double-edged Sword
Double Meaning
Double Standard
Double Trouble

IN COMMON
Common Good
Common Ground
Common Sense
Common Area
Shared
Mutual
Joint
Lowest Common Denominator
Mutually Exclusive

PROBABILITY and POSSIBILITY
Chance
Odds
Impossible (0%)
Extremely Unlikely / Improbable
Equally Likely (50%)
Likely
Extremely Likely / Probable
Certain / Definite / Guaranteed

USEFUL PHRASES FOR GUESSING POSSIBILITIES
It could / couldn't be
It might / might not be
It's probably / probably not
It must be / It must not be
It can / can't be... (because)
It's almost certainly / certainly not
It's definitely / definitely not
It's absolutely / absolutely not
It could possibly be

PREFIX - "DIS"
Dislike
Disapprove
Dishonest
Disbelief
Distrust
Disembowel *does not fit the pattern
Disinfect
Disrespect

PREFIX - "UN"
Unsafe
Uncool
Uncomfortable
Unfair
Unzip
Uneasy *does not fit the pattern
Unimportant
Unintended
Unlikely

PREFIX - "RE"
Repay
Return
Reappear
Review
Recover
Require
Rearrange
Remove
Reject*

PREFIX - "PRE"
Preschool
Prevent
Preview
Precaution
Predict
Prepay
Premature
Predetermined
Pretense
Preexisting

APPENDIX B: CHESS PERFORMANCE.

[*Trumpet fanfare plays.* Black King (BK), comes out limping with a cane a la Willy Wonka. Slowly limps forward until cane drops and he does a perfect forward roll and stands up with arms outstretched to applause from the audience and all the other pieces]

[Black Queen (BQ) approaches]

BQ - Well that was magnificent. You sure do know how to make an entrance, your majesty! Say, I was thinking, how about I stand on the black square today? After all, you know that color goes so well with my outfit! I really think I should stand on my own color!

BK - I love you, darling, but you know how everyone always says I'm the most important piece in the game?

BOARD [Aside, to audience] - He's right, everyone is always saying that.

BK - Well, I think the most important piece in the game should stand wherever he wants.

BQ - But your majesty, haven't you gotten bored...

BOARD - [Aside, to audience, points to himself] - Did someone say board?!?

BQ - [Sassy, aside to BOARD and audience] - Actually, yes, I did say "bored" but bored is a homonym, which if you didn't know, is a word that sounds the same when you say it but is spelled differently and also has another meaning altogether. So in fact, when I just said "bored" I was referring to a general sense of ennui and disinterest owing to repetition, B-O-R-E-D, not you, the chess board, B-O-A-R-D.

BOARD - Oh.

BQ - Anyway, as I was saying, your majesty, haven't you gotten bored of standing on your own color? I know I eventually get bored of the same thing. Maybe we can change positions?

BK - Darling, I would really prefer to stay on the black square today. Isn't that OK with you? [sings] Don't you… love me?

BQ - [To herself and audience] Do I love him? [To audience, singing] Do I looooove you?

[*Melody from Fiddler on The Roof song, "Do You Love Me?"*]
For hundreds of years I've been your bride
Been your queen, fought and died
Been sa-cri-ficed to the other siiiiide,
And because of your pride, you still cannot stand asiiide…

BK - Ugh, I can't have this conversation right now. Cloooooooock!!! [Chess clock appears] Oh look, the clock is showing time. Time to go dance with the Rook!

BOARD - What he's referring to is called castling. [BK and R demonstrate as BOARD explains] You see, in order to be better protected, once the light pieces are developed out of the way, the king can "do a dance" with a Rook, the Rook slides over and the King slides behind and around.

BISHOPS (BB) and (WB) and KNIGHT - Did somebody say light pieces?!?

BOARD - [annoyed] I said it.

BQ - Did you know that "light" is not a homonym, but rather a homograph? That's a word which is spelled and sounds the same, but has several different meanings. Other examples of homographs are "bark", "tie", "wave"....

WHITE BISHOP (WB) - Excuse me, grammar queen, but I believe we were about to be introduced.

BOARD - [annoyed] sigh OK, sometimes I feel like everyone is constantly walking all over me. You guys introduce yourselves.

WB and BB - [together] We are the bishops. We have pointy things, kind of like unicorns.

BB - I am a black, light square bishop. Not a black dark square bishop.

WB - And I am a white, dark square bishop. Not a white light square bishop.

WB and BB [exchange glances, together] - That's kind of confusing. Is that right? Yes, I think it's right.

BOARD - Yes, that's right. Each side has two bishops in the game. A light square, and a dark square bishop. They move and capture diagonally, along their own color squares.

ALL TOGETHER - A light square bishop and a dark square bishop will always stay on their own color the entire game. They are like cats and dogs. Just like a dog can never become a cat, and a cat can never become a dog, the light square bishop can never become a dark square bishop, and a dark square bishop can never become a light square bishop.

WB and WB - [face, and to each other] I want be you, but I can't.

ROOK - Ahem, I just want to slide in here and explain that, I too, like the bishops, can move as many squares as I want, except I don't move diagonally, but rather side to side on the ranks --

BOARD -- those are the horizontal [ALL - make arm gesture] paths on the board

ROOK -- and up and down on the files --

BOARD -- those are the vertical [ALL - make arm gesture] paths on the board.

CHESS CLOCK - OK, OK that's enough. Can we get on with it. I feel like we're running out of time, it'll be night soon.

KN - [Jumps] Did someone say knight?!?

BQ - Actually, "knight" is also a homonym because --

ALL TOGETHER - Oooookaaaaaay!!! We get it!!!

KN - Anyway, as I was about to say, the knight is the only piece in the game that can jump over other pieces! I am a light piece, just like the bishops, and you should develop me first. I move in a letter L shape, and when I move, I'll always end up on a different color square than the one I started on. On the first move of the game, I'm the only piece you can move that's not a pawn! That's because I can [jumps] jump! and I don't even need the pawns to move out of the way!

PAWN - Did someone say pawn?

BOARD - Aren't there supposed to be eight of you? Where are the other seven?

PAWN - Oh, you mean Dopey, Sneezy, Bashful, Sleepy, Happy, Grumpy and Doc? They got held up at the pawn shop.

ALL TOGETHER - [Groooooooooooan]

BOARD - [shakes his head and rolls his eyes] You guys are supposed to be a team! You're supposed to be here to tell us about how the pawns move and capture.

PAWN - Well, you don't need all eight of us to tell you that. Everyone already knows, right guys?

ALL TOGETHER - Pawns move only forward, and on their first move they can advance one or two squares. After that, only one square at a time. They capture diagonally, like the bishops --

BISHOPS - That's us!

ALL TOGETHER -- but only one square diagonally to the right or left.

PAWN - Aren't you guys gonna tell them about that special thing that I can do?

ALL TOGETHER - when a pawn advances all the way to the other side of the board, it can transform, or "be promoted", to any other piece, except the king.

BQ - Ahem. Usually, but not always, you'd want to promote your pawn to a Queen, since I am the most powerful piece in the game.

ALL TOGETHER - a pawn that advances - or is about to advance - to the other side, is called a passed pawn.

CLOCK - Did someone say Spassky?

BOARD - No… I don't think so.

BQ - Actually, "passed" is also a homonym --

BOARD - Sometimes I feel like I just want to resign.

CLOCK - [in Russian, from Wikipedia] Бори́с Васи́льевич Спа́сский советский и французский шахматист, 10-й чемпион мира по шахматам (1969—1972). Международный гроссмейстер (1955), заслуженный мастер спорта СССР (1965)[3]. Двукратный чемпион СССР (1961, 1973), десятикратный участник шахматных олимпиад. В 1972 году он проиграл матч Роберту Фишеру. он усовершенствовал дебютный репертуар, позиционное мастерство и эндшпильную технику и в период расцвета был универсальным игроком, исключительно сильным во всех компонентах игры.

ALL - [stare at clock]

BB - Hey CLOCK, where did you learn all that?

CLOCK - Tik Tok.

ALL TOGETHER - [Grooooooooooan]

ROOK - Hey guys, you're forgetting the most important part.

KN - Sorry, did we jump ahead?

ROOK - Well, yes. [Clears throat] I just want to say something about my dance partner here. [Soft piano music plays, Rook walks along the stage slowly] You see, you can't just talk about the beautiful game of chess without talking about the object of the game. The way to win is to trap your opponent's king, so that he's under attack [ALL TOGETHER - That's a check!], but unable to escape. A king cannot be captured and taken off the board, so a checkmate ends the game. [ALL TOGETHER - Checkmate!].

[*Bowie's Let's Dance* plays, Rook and King join hands and begin dancing, everyone joins in for choreographed dance].

ABOUT THE AUTHOR

Sasha Yevelev was born in the former Soviet Union in 1982. He was a sickly child, and spent a lot of time in Soviet hospitals where he learned to make paper guns and paper airplanes. In 1990, he immigrated to San Jose, California, with his parents, grandmother, and two brothers. The first time he tasted Pepsi was at the airport in Toronto - a stopover on that trip out of the USSR. Despite this transformative experience, he doesn't drink soda today. When he was 11 years old, Sasha had a short entrepreneurial stint selling peanut brittle and emergency candles. He spent most of the money at the arcade, getting really good at Street Fighter II. He was the first person in his family to have a Bar Mitzvah, and the first to visit Israel.

After graduating with a B.S. in Business Administration from The Haas School of Business at The University of California, Berkeley, he went to find himself in Europe for about three months. Then he returned, and dabbled with various roles in the corporate world. Eventually he decided to continue the family legacy of photography, and, following in his grandfather's footsteps, he began a career as a professional photographer in 2006. Sasha has photographed over 1,000 weddings, and thus, over 2,000 pairs of wedding shoes.

His father Igor is a published poet and author; his mother Dina has published her own cookbook; his brother Gary has helped prepare published legal opinions; his brother Ed has published books of political cartoons. Therefore, he is the last person in his family to publish anything of consequence.

ABOUT THE DESIGNER

Ed Yevelev is an illustrator, cartoonist, graphic designer, and competitive pun-maker based in the East Bay, California. He started drawing at the age of seven, while also voraciously reading Calvin and Hobbes and Far Side comics.

Ed launched his amateur political cartooning career as an editorial cartoonist for UC Berkeley's independent student newspaper, The Daily Californian. He received multiple student journalism awards and even more hate mail. He published his first book of political cartoons about Donald Trump, *Little Drawcket Man*, in 2018.

A recovering sports journalist, Ed has taken his puns to the marketing world while rooting for Cal and the Warriors. You can follow his latest work at edyevelevcartoons.com and @edyevelevcartoons on Instagram.

www.ingramcontent.com/pod-product-compliance
Lightning Source LLC
LaVergne TN
LVHW010621100826
845148LV00014B/3061

* 9 7 8 1 7 3 6 7 3 2 6 0 1 *